D1635814

William M. Clarke

How the City of London Works

An Introduction to its Financial Markets

5th Edition

First Edition 1986
2nd Edition 1988
3rd Edition 1991
4th Edition 1995
Reprinted 1996
5th Edition 1999
W. M. Clarke 1986, 1988, 1991, 1995, 1999

*Published in 1999 by Sweet and Maxwell Limited of
100 Avenue Road, London NW3 3PF
Computerset by Wyvern 21 Ltd, Bristol
Printed in England by Clays Ltd, St Ives plc.*

No natural forests were destroyed to make this product, only farmed
timber was used and replanted

**A CIP catalogue record for this book is available from the
British Library**

ISBN 0 421 652705

By the Same Author

The Letters of Wilkie Collins
The Lost Fortune of the Tsars
Planning for Europe: 1992
The Secret Life of Wilkie Collins
Inside the City
The World's Money
Britain's Invisible Earnings
Private Enterprise in Developing Countries
The City in the World Economy
The City's Invisible Earnings

Preface

The aim of this small guide is to explain quite simply what goes on in the financial markets of the City of London and how each of them works. It is intended, therefore, as a helpful companion to the stream of other books on the City's activities.

It is not concerned with the arguments about the City: whether it does harm to the economy or whether it is the saviour of Britain's balance of payments. It is in essence a "child's guide" (in words, diagrams and pictures) to the score of markets and specialisations that make up London's financial centre.

I am once again indebted to all the leading City institutions and associations for the helpful provision of both material and time in the preparation of this small book.

W.M.C.
April 1999

Contents

To Deborah, Pamela, Evan and Noel

1. What the City Does

Where it is

Before trying to describe how the City works, let's first establish where it is. As its nickname suggests, it covers no more than a square mile (actually 274 hectares) and is roughly synonymous with the local authority area of the Corporation of London.

It is hardly a square, more an odd-shaped rectangle, stretching from the Law Courts at one end to the Tower of London at the other, and from the north bank of the Thames in the south to the outskirts of the Barbican and Liverpool Street Station, in the north.

Within its narrow area, the various markets and specialisations cluster in quite separate spots, banking here, insurance there, commodities here, shipping over there. Yet none is far from the others. It is possible to walk from one end of the City to the other in under twenty minutes and most of the main sections are within five minutes' walk of each other.

Where then to start? The obvious spot is Bank tube station. As one emerges from the exit in front of the Royal Exchange steps one is at the heart of the financial district. The Royal Exchange has been the home, in the course of its four hundred year history, of Lloyd's, the foreign exchange market, LIFFE financial futures market, several commodity markets and Guardian insurance group, one of the oldest of the insurance companies.

Over on the left is the entrance to the Bank of England. A little beyond in the same direction rises the Stock Exchange tower. Immediately behind one is the Mansion House, home (literally) of the Lord Mayor. And, within two hundred years in different directions, stand the headquarters of the big clearing banks: Lloyds (on the right, just across Cornhill), Barclays, Midland, National Westminster and the London office of the Royal Bank of Scotland.

This, therefore, is the hub of the financial district, with various spokes of the wheel leading off to the commodity markets, between

1

Fenchurch Street and Eastcheap, the insurance broking world, extending from Leadenhall Street and Lime Street towards Aldgate, the shipping community around Leadenhall Street and St Mary Axe, and the discount house close to Lombard Street, with foreign banks clustered down Gresham Street, Moorgate and now Eastcheap.

What it does

The phrase "the City of London" is employed as useful shorthand to describe the financial (and commercial) institutions in the Square Mile; and, like all shorthand phrases, it leaves out a great deal. It should not imply that other cities in the United Kingdom do not have similar institutions. Nor should it leave the impression that most people employed in finance actually work in London (in fact, only about a fifth do so).

Bank branches operate in most high streets. So do thousands of insurance company branches, insurance brokers and unit trust offices. Edinburgh rivals London as the hub of the investment trust world and Birmingham, Manchester, Liverpool, Leeds, Newcastle and Bristol are commercial centres in their own right.

What then distinguishes London from the rest? Fundamentally it is that the main financial markets operate in the Square Mile and that the head offices of most financial institutions are still located there. It is also the home of the Government's main monetary arm, the Bank of England, and the place where foreign financial institutions choose to place their representatives.

For all these reasons, London's markets and institutions attract the bulk of the country's savings, investments and money decisions in general. Thus the City is like some huge magnet, pulling the results of activities in Manchester, Birmingham or even Hong Kong or Rio to a narrow spot in London, whether they relate to foreign exchange, rubber, shipping freights, satellite risks, Government securities, or just the payment of a bill by cheque. In one way or another, the City's mechanism comes into play.

London's Markets

Let us be more precise. A good many people, in the course of their working life, make contributions to their future pensions on a regular basis. Their employer, who will also be making a contribution, will have a pension fund to receive such contributions and to invest the money as it accumulates. How is this done? The fund will have an investment manager who in turn will use a stockbroker or investment banker to help him choose and purchase industrial shares, gilt-edged stock or even foreign securities. Such transactions will ultimately lead to the purchase of existing, or sometimes newly issued, stock in the stock market. So at the end of the chain, a transaction takes place in the market-place in the City of London.

Also consider the sale of British machinery in Lancashire to a foreign importer in Mexico. The transaction will need to be financed, insured and shipped. A local bank in Manchester will arrange export finance through its foreign branch in London; insurance may be arranged through a London-based company; and the shipping arrangements may eventually be secured on the Baltic Exchange in St Mary Axe. City institutions, not a stone's throw from each other, enable the transaction to be completed.

Finally, take an endowment policy taken out with a life insurance office in Norwich, Salisbury or Gloucester. The premiums will be paid annually. The life office needs to invest the money until either a death claim is made or the policy matures; and it will consider a number of options: buying industrial equities or Government securities; purchasing farmland or property; investing abroad in existing shares or in a wide range of venture enterprises. The decisions to do one or the other will inevitably take place in the life company's London office and that office, in turn, will use the appropriate City market for its purposes: the stock market to buy securities; the foreign exchange market to transfer funds abroad for foreign investment or to cover some of its risks; even the new financial futures market to cover some of its other risks.

To sum up

Once again a small transaction in the provinces has led to the use of markets or specialisations in the City. We shall discover more examples as we go along. But, at this early stage, let us try to sum up what the City, in its broadest sense, seems to do:

(i) It enables monetary payments to be made from one person (or company) to another.

(ii) It enables payments to be made across frontiers to and from any country in the world.

(iii) It attracts investment funds from all parts of the United Kingdom and overseas and, through its markets and contacts, provides a means of investing them in securities, industrial plant, property, farmland, commodities or gold.

(iv) It provides the means of financing trade, industry and government projects on a national or world-wide basis.

(v) It offers a variety of financial and commercial services on an international scale, from insurance to shipping freights and from investment advice to legal advice.

In short, it will save, invest, finance, insure, ship, trade, buy, sell or hedge for you, me, or anyone else, on a world-wide basis. How it does so, we must begin to explore in the next chapter.

The City's Dockland Extension

The fiscal attractions offered by the Docklands Development Corporation and the modern accommodation increasingly available have combined to produce a potential extension of the City two miles east of the City. The multi-billion development is filling up with British and, mainly, American financial institutions, such as Morgan Stanley, Credit Suisse First Boston, and the Financial Services Authority. They will also be joined by Citibank, HSBC and Salomon Smith Barney. The 800-foot, 50-storey tower at Canary Wharf, Britain's tallest, has already become a feature of the City's eastern skyline, and is capable of housing 11,500 office workers. Present expansion plans include two new 42-storey towers.

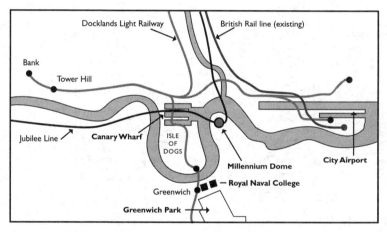

Some people believe it will shift the City's centre of gravity eastwards and create similar transport problems in London to those faced by visiting bankers in New York, in coping with offices in both Lower Manhattan and Park Avenue. More likely, the City's "decision-making" fulcrum will remain around the Bank of England and Dockland will become an exciting, integrated extension of the City's new market-dealing floor technology, linked to the City by new roads, Light Railway and the Jubilee Line.

Where To See The City at Work

The following walk through the City, calling at some of the markets, is designed to provide a visual impression of what the City really stands for: active markets in money, goods and services. They provide the same colour, bustle and noise of markets anywhere, with one major difference: the prices are rather higher.

Several parts of the City and its markets can still be visited. But it is no longer the easy arrangement it used to be. Some markets, such as the Stock Exchange, have been replaced by computer screens in offices. Some remain closed. Others, such as the Bank of England Museum, the London Metal Exchange and the Baltic Exchange cannot cope with large numbers. So appointments and forward planning are essential.

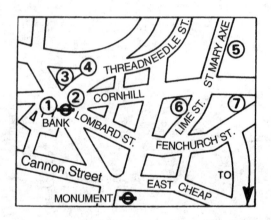

WE START AT BANK UNDERGROUND STATION

[←]

(1) Mansion House

The Mansion House is the official residence of the Lord Mayor of London. It is also the venue for much of the City's hospitality where guests such as the Prime Minister, Chancellor of the Exchequer, foreign Heads of State, etc., are invited to official banquets. The building was started in 1738 and completed in 1752. The Lord Mayor is titular head of the Corporation of London, the City's governing body, which is responsible through its elected members for the administration of the City, providing, in essence, the infrastructure for the financial sector.

[�]

(2) Royal Exchange

In the past, the Royal Exchange has housed the City's foreign exchange market and Lloyd's. At present it is the home of the Guardian insurance group. The present building was opened by Queen Victoria on October 28, 1844. Royal Exchange Assurance, now merged in the Guardian insurance group, have occupied the building (and its two predecessors) since 1720, though they move in the near future. The London International Financial Futures and Options Exchange occupied the area of the courtyard and ambulatory in the 1980s before moving to other premises.

[➤]

(3) Bank of England

Founded in 1694, the Bank of England did not move into Threadneedle Street until 1734. The nickname "The Old Lady of Threadneedle Street" was first used in James Gillray's cartoon of 1797. The Bank expanded to cover the present site between 1765 and 1833, and was finally rebuilt by Sir Herbert Baker between 1925 and 1939. In the vaults are the nation's gold reserves.

[➤]

(4) London Stock Exchange

The London Stock Exchange has its origins in the sixteenth century and as the scale of commercial activity has increased, especially in the last 150 years, the Exchange has expanded to handle the increased demand for capital. The present building was opened by the Queen in November 1972.

[➤]

(5) Baltic Exchange

The former Baltic Exchange was destroyed by IRA bombing in 1992 and is now in new premises in St Mary Axe. It is a unique international shipping exchange. Its members comprise merchants, ship-owners, shipbrokers and other companies associated with shipping. It regards itself as the only self-regulated international freight market in the world. About 1,500 nominated representatives trade in the market but business is mainly done between offices. Other members include maritime lawyers, financiers and arbitrators.

[➡]

(6) Lloyd's

Lloyd's of London is an international insurance market. Insurance risks are placed with a mix of individual underwriting members with unlimited liability and corporate members trading with limited liability who, together, provide the capital base for 139 syndicates. Business from all parts of the world is placed at Lloyd' through the 170 authorised firms of Lloyd's brokers. Its new building was opened in November 1986.

[➡]

(7) London Metal Exchange

The London Metal Exchange is an international terminal market where copper, lead, zinc, tin, aluminium, aluminium alloy and nickel are trade in standard units of guaranteed quality. Trade is conducted inter-office and by open outcry, the latter involving the 14 Ring firms who representatives call out their offers for sale and bids to buy in four sessions each day. The market moved in 1994 to prestigious new premises at 56, Leadenhall Street.

[➡]

RETURN TO MONUMENT UNDERGROUND STATION

List of Addresses and Contact Point

Guildhall

Members of the public may visit the Great Hall from 09.00 – 16.00, Monday to Friday. Visitors who wish to tour Guildhall with a Guide must contact the Keeper's Office. Anyone wishing to visit a Livery Company should contact the individual company direct.

Where to Write:

Keeper's Office
Corporation of London
PO Box 270 Guildhall
London EC2P 2EJ Tel:
0207 332 1460

Mansion House

Groups may be shown round Mansion House by appointment.

Where to Write:

Principal Assistant to
the Lord Mayor
Mansion House
London EC4N 8BH
Tel: 0207 626 2500

Bank of England Museum

Admission is free. Educational presentations take place in the Bank of England's Museum cinema (entrance in Bartholomew Lane), and are for groups of between 12 and 30 people, although smaller groups may be accepted in exceptional circumstances. Bookings must be arranged in advance. Museum open Monday to Friday (10–5 p.m.) and presentations at 10.00 a.m., 11.00 a.m., 12.00 a.m., 2.00 p.m. and 3.00 p.m. The groups catered for are:

(1) 5–10-year-olds. A 60-minute presentation is given, taking the audience on a trip through time, stopping to look at different systems of exchange and money. There will be some audience participation and a 15-minute cartoon film, *The Curious History of Money.*
Allow 2 hours for visit. One hour for museum.

(2) 11–14-year-olds. A 60-minute presentation is given, looking in very simple terms at the qualities of money, including colour slides and a cartoon film.
Allow 1 hour for visit.

(3) 15 + years. A 20-minute film on the Bank and its various activities, followed by a question and answer session.
Allow 45 minutes to 1 hour for visit.

(4) General interest. A 60-minute slide show can be seen, covering the history and work of the Bank of England.
Allow 1 hour for visit.

Where to Write:

Secretary's Department
Bank of England
Threadneedle Street
London EC2R 8AH
Museum enquiries and
tours: 0207 601 5491
Educational groups:
0207 601 3985

London Stock Exchange

The Stock Exchange closed for public viewing in 1990.

Where to Write:

Enquiries: Proshare:
0207 216 8812 London
Stock Exchange: 0207
588 2355

9

Baltic Exchange

By appointment only. Small groups with specific interest in international bulk shipping.

Where to Write:

The Chief Executive The Baltic Exchange St Mary Axe London EC3A 8BH Tel: 0207 369 1621

Lloyd's

Visiting facilities are available for pre-booked parties only. Charges are made for visits.

Where to Write:

Corporate Communications Department Lloyd's of London 1 Lime Street London EC3M 7HA Tel: 0171 623 7100

London Metal Exchange

The public may arrange to watch the "Ring" by appointment. Most visits are from 12 noon to 1.00 p.m. and video presentations are available. Parties should number no more than 15. Those taking part must be of at least "A" level standard.

Where to Write:

The Marketing Department London Metal Exchange 56 Leadenhall Street London EC3A 2DX Tel: 0207 264 5555

2. Banking

What is Money?

Money is at the heart of the City, and so are the banks which deal in money and, to some extent, even create it.

In order to know what a bank is and does, therefore, we need to know a little about the developments in the use of money: how in brief we managed to move from barter to the creation of credit. This was, of course, achieved in two basic stages. First came the transition from barter to the use of shells, beads and gold as a means of exchange: that is, the creation of acceptable, though often primitive, money. This in turn led to the establishment of coins and, much later, paper notes by governments and, more recently, to the use of telephonic and electronic transfers of money. The second stage, which overlapped the first, was the jump from an acceptable means of exchange to the creation of credit; and then, in progression, to the use of cheques, credit cards, electronic money and home banking by television.

Let us begin with money itself. As the textbooks always tell us, money is simply an acceptable means of exchange that can be measured in small units, and used as a stable store of value. The key word is acceptable. People must be willing to accept the means of exchange, whether beads, shells or paper notes, knowing that when the time comes to exchange them, in their turn, for something else, their value will be universally recognised.

A bank is not necessary for this basic mechanism of exchange. What a bank is useful for (though not entirely necessary for, as we shall see in a moment) is the next step in development: the creation of credit. Historically, credit creation can be pushed back as far as the Florentines in the 15th century. But it was being undertaken on a regular basis by the goldsmiths by the end of the seventeenth century; they were well-established as safe havens not only for bullion, but jewellery and cash. They had also begun to do something else, which was to

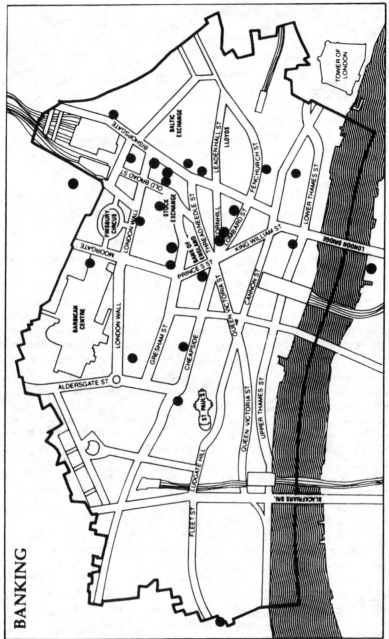

BANKING

TOWER OF LONDON

BISHOPSGATE
BALTIC EXCHANGE
LEADENHALL ST
LLOYDS
FENCHURCH ST
LOWER THAMES ST
OLD BROAD ST
STOCK EXCHANGE
THREADNEEDLE ST
CORNHILL
LOMBARD ST
KING WILLIAM ST
LONDON BRIDGE
FINSBURY CIRCUS
LONDON WALL
BANK OF ENGLAND
PRINCE S ST
MOORGATE
QUEEN VICTORIA ST
CANNON ST
BARBICAN CENTRE
LONDON WALL
GRESHAM ST
CHEAPSIDE
QUEEN VICTORIA ST
QUEEN THAMES ST
UPPER THAMES ST
ALDERSGATE ST
ST PAUL'S
LUDGATE HILL
BLACKFRIARS BRI.
FLEET ST

● *Main U.K. banking locations (original source: Savills).*

12

have a much wider significance: they started to issue receipts for such deposits and to lend some of the wealth left with them to others.

The receipts rapidly developed into bank notes and the lending of the deposited money (at least up to certain proportions which they learned to be safe) took them into banking as we now know it. They were, in essence, judging how much of their basic deposits would be needed soon, and lending the rest to people whom they felt were credit-worthy.

But one need not seek such credit-creating examples in history. Just consider what happened in Ireland's pubs when the banks closed during a prolonged strike in the 1960s. Here is a contemporary description by Lord Kilbracken of one Irish village, Killeshandra:

"The first thing that happened was that most grocers and almost all pubs became bankers overnight. They were taking lots of money which they didn't like keeping in cash.

So they were happy to change cheques much more readily than usual. They also made many arrangements with local factories and offices which took no cash but required it for wages.

The money taken across the counter at Looney's Bar was sent down the road to pay the wages at O'Rourke's factory.

Then things went a stage further. Looney would receive in return O'Rourke's unencashable cheque. But the credit standing of Seamus O'Rourke is good, and it would be accepted by the wholesaler in payment of Looney's account.

The wholesaler, in return, would pass it on, till eventually it might find its way back to Seamus, who could happily tear it up."

So a nation managed to live on existing credit (cheques circulated through pubs, grocers, etc.) for several months without a bank being open. Whether it could have continued to do so much longer, without a major disaster, is open to doubt. The example simply serves to show that, even without a bank, credit is based on acceptability, trust and the judgement of credit-worthiness.

What is a Bank?

We can now return to the real banking world, and reconsider what a bank is and does. Amazingly, despite London being regarded as a major banking centre, no definition existed of a bank prior to 1979. At that time a Banking Act was passed resulting from the secondary banking collapse of the 1970s. The Act defined a bank and established a two-tier status. The largest banks, providing a comprehensive range of services, were known as recognised banks, whilst smaller and more specialised institutions were known as licensed deposit takers. The 1979 Banking Act made it illegal for anybody not authorised to accept deposits from the general public. The two-tier system was abolished by the Banking Act 1987 and now there is a single category of "authorised institutions" which can vary from Barclays Bank to the financial subsidiary of Marks and Spencer.

How then does a bank move from that first step of the acceptance of a monetary deposit from the public to the creation of credit? If it wishes to survive it will wish to invest its first deposits in ways that secure a steady income and still enable it to pay back its depositors on demand, or when agreed. This will persuade it to lend some of it on a day-to-day basis in the money market and to acquire short-term Government bonds. It will also, particularly if it is a High Street bank, leave some on deposit at the Bank of England—the equivalent of cash. All this ensures that its essential "liquidity" (that is, its ability to turn the investments into cash quickly) remains high.

Over time the banks will have learnt that some depositors are longer-term than others and, like the goldsmiths, they will consider on-lending some of these deposits to commercial borrowers. Thus begins the pyramid of credit creation we are all familiar with.

In fact, when a bank agrees to make a loan it does not usually dole out the whole amount in cash. The borrower is able to overdraw his normal account (made up of the money he has deposited with the bank) by the use of a cheque book. These cheques will, in their turn, be deposited in a bank. As a result, unless an overdraft is being repaid, total deposits are increased as a result of the new loan. Loans are created in more direct ways too.

Similarly if a bank buys securities it will provide a cheque in exchange and this too will eventually be deposited in a bank. Here again total deposits will have been increased. Thus both new loans and the purchase of new securities often lead to the creation of deposits. These are just examples of the way in which deposits can be created by individual banks. The process also embraces the banking system as a whole.

The only brake on this magical process, apart from the Bank of England's constant supervision, is, of course, the banks' fear that its original depositors (as well as the new ones) will want their money back in the form of cash. If they did, there would be what is known as a "run on the bank", customers rushing to get their money back at the same time. To avoid this banks have learned to maintain a certain level of cash (in notes and coins or with the Bank of England) or other liquid assets which can be turned into cash quickly.

We can now see how and why a bank uses its resources in a variety of ways, keeping some in cash or "near-cash" (*i.e.* a deposit at the Bank of England), investing some short-term in bills or loans to the money market, investing some in Government securities of varying lengths, and lending some to personal and corporate borrowers.

What banks offer

So far we have explained that banks receive deposits and invest and lend the proceeds. These different processes now need to be explained in a little more detail.

The reasons why banks receive deposits are not far to seek. A current account provides the customer with the means of making payments swiftly and efficiently, by the use of cheques, standing orders or credit transfers. A deposit account is a way of keeping money safe, and, at the same time, earning interest. Banks now offer a variety of options to depositors, varying from bank to bank, and ranging from small savings and budget accounts to so-called deposit accounts for especially large sums. They also entice customers with a variety of services, from the safeguarding of valuables (shades of the goldsmiths) to executor and trustee services.

There is one further source of deposits which needs to be sketched in before we turn to the uses banks make of them. Until about twenty years ago, the main commercial banks relied almost entirely on normal short-term deposits for their various lending activities. But with the abolition of their agreed rates of interest (at which each bank received deposits) they were able to compete individually for large sums of money from other financial institutions and elsewhere. From that moment onwards each bank offered to pay its own agreed rates of interest over agreed periods. On this basis a new highly competitive inter-bank money market was established. It was, in effect, a large wholesale money market and enabled the banks to offer medium-term loans. With some money lent to them for longer periods, the banks were able to offer loans for longer periods too.

Let us now turn to the use made of all these deposits. We have already touched on the various ways in which the banks invest their money in the money market, the gilt-edged market and the Bank of England. We shall be explaining exactly how they do this and what effect it has on official monetary policy when we look at the operations of the money market in Chapter 7.

This brings us to their lending policies and the different methods they use to provide loans to customers. This can best be tackled by brief descriptions of what they offer.

Overdrafts The overdraft is the traditional British method of obtaining short-term funds for personal convenience or, in business, often to finance stocks or work in progress. The customer agrees a maximum limit with his bank and can then draw on his own account up to this amount, being charged only on what he uses at the current rate of interest. The overdraft has flexibility, for the bank and customer, but it is also repayable on demand. Although banks normally agree to "roll over" overdrafts (*i.e.* to lengthen the term of the loan, after appropriate reviews, by extensions), it is not a satisfactory way of providing industry with longer-term certainty.

Term Loans   These are basically for a fixed amount, for a fixed period (say seven to ten years though sometimes up to 25 or 30 years) and at a fixed or variable rate of interest for the purchase of fixed assets such as premises or machinery. The borrower can receive the whole amount at once or draw it down gradually and naturally pays for it from the first day. The borrower does not have the full flexibility provided by an overdraft, though he can still choose when he needs the money. He has the advantage of knowing it is his for the agreed period and he can plan accordingly. It is worth noting that a contractual loan of this kind can also be for a short period.

Consumer Finance   Whilst overdrafts have been the traditional method of obtaining finance from a bank in this country, tremendous growth has been seen in the provision to private customers of packaged lending. This consists of personal loans, revolving credit accounts and budget accounts and in addition many banks are moving towards formal overdraft arrangements linked to income levels and renewable on an annual basis.

All the banks provide credit card facilities to customers and non-customers alike. Banks have also encroached on the traditional business of building societies, house mortgage lending.

Financial Services   As the financial markets have been deregulated, the banks have diversified into the provision of a vast range of financial services. Banks today represent a substantial proportion of new insurance policies and unit trusts sold.

Export Credits   Financing international trade, through the use of the traditional overdraft (see p. 15) or the acceptance credit (see p. 17), has been the accepted role of the banks for well over a century. The main domestic banks, however, moved into the financing of overseas trade only this century. The variations are now both sophisticated and almost bewildering. In some areas of the world the basic re-assurance needed by banks providing such credits is invariably a Government guarantee covering the political (and allied credit) risk. If the exporter has taken out an insurance policy with the Export Credits Guarantee Department (ECGD), and assigned it to the bank concerned, it provides collateral for the essential credit.

Bills of Exchange These have been the traditional instrument used in international trade for centuries, though their use is now less prevalent. A bill is a promise to pay a given sum on a given date and will often be provided by an importer, while he awaits delivery of the goods. The exporter who receives such a bill can negotiate an overdraft or credit facility with a bank or can discount it, that is sell it to the bank at a discount: another alternative is for the importer to ask his local bank to open what is called a documentary acceptance credit in favour of the exporters; the bank thus promises to accept a bill of exchange accompanied by shipping documents. Acceptance credits have traditionally been offered as a form of short-term credit by London's accepting houses (another word for the merchant banks), when they "accept" bills of exchange. This means that they guarantee payment of the bill on the due date, in return for a commission. Such bank bills (*i.e.* with the name of a bank on them) can be discounted in the money market.

Factoring Exporters or other traders with trade debts of varying kinds can offer them to a bank providing factoring services and receive various services. The bank (or factoring subsidiary) will relieve the exporter of the debt anxieties, provide a sales ledger accounting service and act as debt-collector. The exporter will often be provided with cash for his day-to-day needs.

Leasing Banks, or their leasing subsidiaries, finance the acquisition of equipment, machinery, vehicles, etc., through leasing. This means that the assets concerned are hired out, at agreed rates, to the borrowing company but remain in the ownership of the bank or leasing company and revert to them at the end of the agreed period of the lease. Leasing companies (or the banks involved) sometimes provide servicing and maintenance.

Forfeiting This is a form of supplier's credit ranging from six months to five years and above. The mechanism used is the purchase of bills of exchange or promissory notes (rather like IOUs) by the bank in cases where the piece of paper is evidence of deferred trade debt. The bills or notes are usually arranged to mature at six monthly intervals. The bill (or IOU) is regarded as a firm obligation on the part of the importer to pay.

The Banking Habit in Britain

Banking habits continue to change. Though well over 90% of the adult population now have a current account, the banks involved and the way in which payments are made are still developing fast.

The original "High Street" banks, with the familiar bank branch on prominent street corners, have faced stiff competition from the building societies—first outside the fold, now both inside (with Abbey National, Halifax, Woolwich, etc., becoming banks) and outside. Next came the supermarkets and retail chains offering banking services—Tesco, Safeway, Sainsburys, Marks & Spencer, Harrods, Virgin, etc. High Street bank branches have dropped from close on 20,000 in 1990 to around 15,000.

Methods of payment have been changing rapidly too. While the cheque book both replaced cash and complemented it, cash dispensers, especially the 4,000 now installed away from bank branches, provided cash convenience. Credit cards came next—some 37 million in use, accounting for over one billion transactions worth £62 billion at the last count. Now we are offered, and some are using, 24-hour telephone banking (over 3 million customers) and banking by way of computer screens.

Telephone banking already offers a 24-hour service, limited to basic transactions and information, and is provided by several banking institutions. Banking by screen is also developing, by the use of personal computers and television sets, based on software offered by the banks. But the big future breakthrough is clearly the internet, through individual, banking websites. As internet shopping develops apace so, it is expected, will internet banking.

And the next innovation? Probably the introduction of "smart cards", incorporating microchips, offering the services of credit cards, debit cards and "E-money" in one. As for "E-money" (another name for an electronic purse or cash), this facility will be available from a "smart" card loaded with cash amounts, which can then be deducted in small cash amounts as public purchases are made.

Venture Capital The financing of small or new growth enterprises has now expanded into an activity with its own association (the British Venture Capital Association). Venture capital is in essence risk capital coupled with expertise. It can be a combination of equity and fixed interest loans, but the expertise now provided encompasses also acquisitions and management buy-outs (MBOs). The aim behind such financial support for the bank or institution concerned is to enable a small or new company to grow rapidly enough to be sold or floated on an appropriate securities market.

What Merchant and Investment Banks Do

The transformation of the bulk of British merchant banks into international investment banks—some now with American, Swiss, German and French owners—has been one of the major changes in the City's banking structure in recent years. Their ownership has turned full circle. As their names, such as Kleinworts, Hambros, Rothschilds, Schroders, Lazards, etc., imply, most of them began as banking vehicles of a non-British character. London's open attraction to foreign expertise was the driving force behind their creation.

As Britain's political power rose in the late eighteenth century and throughout the nineteenth century, the merchant banks slowly acquired huge financial muscle, lending to individual countries on a large scale and, at the same time, through the unique "Bill on London", oiling a large share of the world's trade. The merchant banks, and their owners, became permanent parts of the London scene and of Britain's establishment.

In the second half of the twentieth century, however, the merchant banks gradually saw their relative financial strength begin to decline, even as they were extending their expertise successfully in new directions. The deposit-raising ability of the big British commercial banks and the huge domestic resources of the American investment banks, now operating in London, dwarfed the amounts the merchant banks could raise from their own or even the capital market's resources.

Other influences were also at work. Although "Big Bang" on the Stock Exchange gave them wider opportunities (see Chapter 4),

(Continued on page 20)

(Continued from page 19)

the Bank of England withdrew some of their discounting privileges and, with growing freedom in financial markets, competition increased. The result was a re-drawing of the banking framework within which former merchant banks, stockbroking and stockjobbing firms, issuing houses and foreign owned investment banks all jostled for position.

What emerged was a typical London compromise in which deposit-raising institutions existed alongside security houses and in some cases merged operations (something that was legally impossible in New York and Tokyo). As globalisation of financial transactions widened international frontiers, it was also natural for the merchant banks to become the targets of the larger foreign groupings: hence the present international ownership of so many of them.

What then do the remaining merchant banks and the enlarged investment banks do? Basically, they undertake wholesale banking business for large industrial and private clients and for Governments and their agencies. Their main areas of activities are now the following:

- *Corporate finance*: offering advice to large corporations on acquisitions, mergers and new issues. This business has reached large proportions and the top banks will regularly advise over 100 large firms each. They will invariably be involved in all major take-over battles.

- *Fund management*: looking after the funds of pension funds, investment and unit trusts, etc., as well as central banks and private individuals, management and advice cover both domestic and international investments (see Chapter 5).

- *Securities trading*: most banks have involved themselves in the business of issuing, and trading in, international bonds and equities (see Chapter 9). Several have come involved in markets in the sovereign debt of developing countries, known as LDC debt trading.

(Continued on page 21)

(Continued from page 20)

● *Banking services*: ranging from foreign exchange business to credits for export business and international projects.

● *Miscellaneous services*: some traditional, some new, embracing property, shipping, timber, commodities, etc. A few are now known as international bullion banks (see Chapter 11).

Which Banks Do What

So far we have talked about banks in general. It is time to be more specific and to explain how they differ and what they all do. Banks can be divided up in several ways. Twenty or thirty years ago the categories would have been different from those we have chosen below. Twenty years ahead, further changes will have taken place. It is worth remembering that we are in effect taking a convenient snapshot of a constantly changing scene. What may seem accurate today may no longer seem so tomorrow.

1. The large *commercial banks*, including former building societies, such as Barclays, Lloyds TSB, Midland (owned by Hong Kong and Shanghai Banking Corporation), National Westminster, Bank of Scotland, Royal Bank of Scotland, Abbey National, Woolwich, Halifax and Alliance & Leicester.
2. *Investment and merchant banks*, with such well known names as Lazards, Rothschilds, Schroders, etc., and Morgan Stanley, Goldman Sachs and Merrill Lynch.
3. *British overseas banks*, such as Standard Chartered, Hong Kong and Shanghai Banking Corporation (formerly in Hong Kong) and Grindlays (now part of the ANZ Banking Group). They have large numbers of branches in overseas territories.
4. *Foreign banks* operating in London through subsidiaries, branches or representative offices. There are now 540 in London.
5. *Nationwide retail banks* offering limited services such as savings, money transfer and other facilities, such as the supermarkets, the National Savings Bank and the National Girobank.

In addition to the above essentially banking structure, there are the *building societies*, which are mutual organisations whose activities are

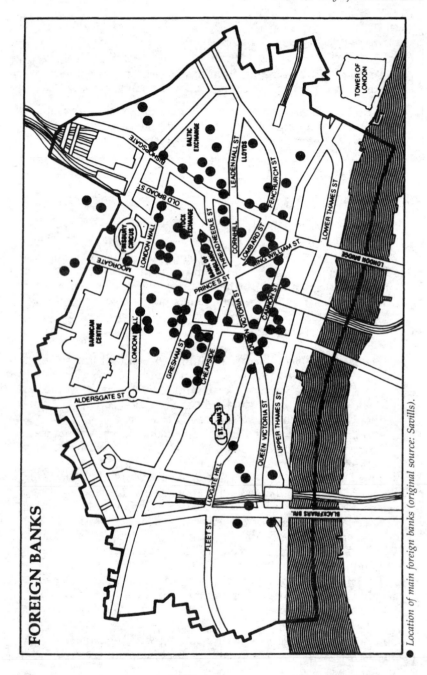

FOREIGN BANKS

controlled by the Building Societies Commission. They were essentially established to attract deposits from individuals on interest-bearing accounts and to provide finance purely for house purchase or home improvements. During the 1970s and 1980s building societies began to offer current-account-type facilities linked to bank accounts, but the Building Societies Act 1986 paved the way for further diversification. As a result, societies can now offer a full range of banking services, including current accounts, cheque cards and credit cards as well as insurance and investment services. This has led to considerable competition between banks and societies, which is likely to intensify. Those that take advantage of the new ability to incorporate themselves and thus become authorised banks, as Abbey National, Woolwich, Cheltenham & Gloucester, Halifax, Alliance & Leicester and Northern Rock have done, will be in direct competition with the banks, with corresponding regional branch networks. Those that do not incorporate the 1986 legislation, coupled with the new liberalisation measures announced in 1994–95, will be allowed to provide several competitive banking services. But for the purposes of this chapter, we have not regarded them as banks. We have also excluded consortium banks, made up of several banks combined for specialised purposes.

It is easier to divide the banks into these five categories than to divide them by their functions. All of them, directly or indirectly, will finance trade and industry, lend money, undertake foreign exchange transactions or give financial advice.

Some are more specialised than others, of course. While the High Street banks are capable of carrying out most kinds of business, they still undertake the bulk of domestic payments and consumer-related transactions. The investment and merchant banks specialise in take-overs and corporate advice, project finance on a world-wide basis, Euro-currency business and investment transactions. The overseas banks and foreign banks naturally specialise in business with their own parts of the world. The foreign banks have been traditionally concerned with trade finance and have been particularly attracted to the Euro-currency market. We shall be considering why in a later chapter.

To sum up, therefore, we can conclude that, in spite of specialisations, there is no longer a clear dividing line between one kind of bank and another. And, as we shall learn shortly in the case of the revolution in the securities market, even the barriers between banking and stockbroking are now becoming more and more blurred.

The Bank of England

The Bank of England remains at the centre of the City, physically and functionally. Its original Royal Charter, granted by King William and Queen Mary in 1694, indicated that it should "promote the Public Good and benefit our people". The Bank now interprets this as maintaining the value of money, ensuring the soundness of the financial system and promoting the efficiency and competitiveness of financial markets.

What it Does

How does it do this? Over the centuries it has accumulated different operational responsibilities and been given political instructions by individual Acts of Parliament—the last two in 1946 and 1998. At present the Bank:

- issues the country's bank notes;
- holds the Government's main bank accounts;
- holds accounts of clearing banks, discount houses, investment and merchant banks, bullion banks, foreign bank, overseas central banks, the International Monetary Fund and a few industrial companies;
- maintains contacts with other central banks and international financial institutions;
- carries out Government monetary policy by its interventions in the money market, gilt-edged market and foreign exchange market;
- has responsibility for maintaining price stability;
- has responsibility for the overall stability of the financial system.

How It Is Run

In 1694, when the bank of England was established, its governing body, the Court of Directors, comprised a Governor, Deputy

(Continued on page 24)

Continued from page 23)

Governor and 24 directors. When it was nationalised (and another Royal Charter granted) in 1946, the number of directors was reduced to 16.

The Bank was ostensibly under Treasury control between 1946 and 1998, since the Treasury could give the Bank such directions as it thought necessary "in the public interest". But this was never in fact implemented and the Bank managed to maintain a discreet independence. The 1998 Act, however, put more clarity into the relationship. The Treasury (in effect the Chancellor) now defines what is meant by "price stability", while the Bank is responsible for maintaining price stability. In other words, the Government sets the inflation target and the Bank takes the operational decisions to achieve it. In addition, the Act established the Monetary Policy Committee as a committee of the Bank, with the Governor as chairman, to formulate and implement monetary policy. In effect this is the body that sets interest rates (see Chapter 7).

How It Operates

In addition to the Governor and two Deputy Governors, the Court of the Bank now includes 16 non-executive directors. Under the Court, the Bank's senior policy-making body is the Governor's Committee made up of the Governor, two Deputy Governors and three executive directors responsible for three areas of operation within the Bank. These areas are:

- *Financial Market Operations* This embraces the operations of the gilt-edged, money and foreign exchange markets, banking services and preparations for the Euro.
- *Financial Stability* This covers markets and trading systems, financial intermediaries, regulatory policy and payments and settlement policy.
- *Monetary Analysis and Statistics* This involves monetary instruments and markets, the preparation of the *Inflation Report*, and economic and monetary analysis and statistics.

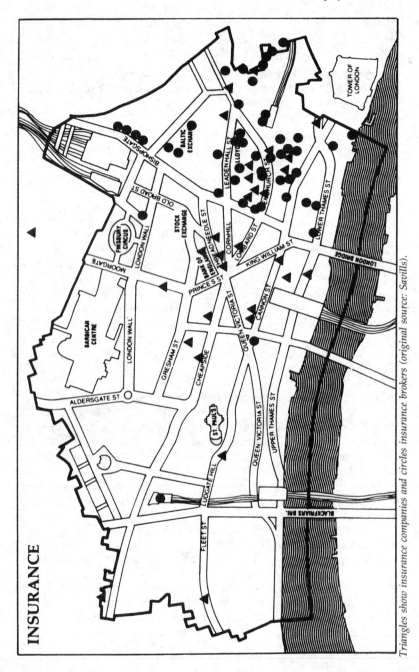

Triangles show insurance companies and circles insurance brokers (original source: Savills).

3. Insurance

What is Insurance?

Insurance, one of the City's oldest activities, is about the sharing of risks. Whether it's the risk of losing your car, your house or your life or the risk of the destruction of a factory, supertanker or even an earth satellite, insurance provides a method of protection.

Insurance works on the principle that not everyone will suffer the same calamity at the same time; and that if we all make a contribution to a communal pool, there will be adequate funds to pay out the main sufferer in full. So by the payment of a sum of money, called the premium, we can be protected against certain specified risks.

Traces of maritime insurance in use in classical Greece and Rome give the industry as lengthy an ancestry as money lending. But, as in the case of banking, the real fundamentals of commercial insurance as we know it emerged much later: marine insurance in the eleventh or twelfth century: fire insurance in the seventeenth century: life assurance in the eighteenth and nineteenth centuries: and aviation and credit insurance in the twentieth century.

Although the terms "assurance" and "insurance" are now interchangeable, they originally had different meanings. "Assurance" was taken out against a risk which was inevitable (*e.g.* death) or the reaching of a particular age, whereas "insurance" was against a risk which might or might not happen.

How it Works

Thus the risks covered by insurance in its broadest sense are basically of two kinds: (i) events which are bound to happen, the date of which is either known or unknown; (ii) events which might or might not happen. In the first category come such things as term or endowment policies, under which money is paid out if a person dies or

25

reaches an agreed age. In the second category are policies under which money is paid out if a car crashes, a house is damaged, or a ship sinks.

In each case the insurance process tends to be much the same. Individual contributions, known as premiums, are paid to the insurance company (or the insurer) by the insured, who receives a policy and is thus known as the policyholder. When (or if) the insured event takes place, a claim is made by the policyholder and a payment is then made out of the insurer's accumulated funds.

These funds are needed to meet such claims and are invested in a variety of ways, depending on the kind of insurance a company specialises in. Companies undertaking life insurance can match some of their investments to the expected pattern of their claims and can invest in longer-term securities.

Companies providing general insurance cover need to have investments which can be turned into cash, without undue loss or delay, and will have some of their money in shorter-term securities.

The Structure

So far we have been concerned with the way in which insurance developed and the principles on which it operates. We must now turn to the main operating participants in the London market. These are:

- Insurance and re-insurance companies;
- Lloyd's;
- Insurance brokers;
- Intermediaries, who also sell insurance.

We need to look at them separately, while bearing in mind throughout that one sector often overlaps with another. Some insurance companies (known as "composite companies") undertake both life and non-life insurance business. Some brokers will provide business both to the companies and to Lloyd's. Some re-insurance companies will undertake general and life business and most insurance companies will undertake re-insurance business.

Insurance Companies

There are now some 841 insurance companies authorised to undertake insurance business in the United Kingdom. Of these, 65 companies transact both life and non-life business (the "composite" companies); 595 specialise in non-life business and 177 are specialist life companies. The big U.K. composite companies include such names as Commercial Union, Eagle Star, Guardian, General Accident, Royal and Sun Alliance. Their main business, at home and abroad, will cover motor, fire, marine, aviation, transport, liability and personal accident classes.

Since some risks, including jumbo jets, industrial projects, oilfields, earthquakes and so on are so great, the process of spreading the risk has had to involve more and more companies. Specialised companies, called re-insurance companies, undertake such spreading of the big risks as their main function. Non-specialised companies as well as Lloyd's also undertake re-insurance. Some risks are so large that only the spreading of them, *i.e.* the re-insuring of them, over hundreds of companies enables such risks to be covered. The San Andreas fault in California and the nightmare of a major earthquake, with losses running into thousands of millions of dollars, is the kind of risk that re-insurance is meant to cope with. Collectively, insurance companies have an annual worldwide premium income of over £120,000 million.

Life Business

As their name implies, these companies concentrate on the provision of life insurance. They include companies, with shareholders, such as Prudential, Pearl and Legal and General, as well as mutual companies basically owned by the policyholders, such as Norwich Union, Equitable Life and the Friends Provident.

The risks they cover can be put quite simply. One out of every four young men now aged 25 will not live to see his 65th birthday. On the other hand, the rest will do so and then need money to retire on. Either way, the man, and his family, will need help to prepare for either eventuality.

Until the middle of the eighteenth century, life insurance as we now know it (that is, based on a detailed analysis of life expectancy tables) did not exist. James Dodson worked out the first tables in 1756, averaging out what a person's annual premiums ought to be, based on patterns of mortality, the laws of averages and the arithmetic of compound interest. But he did not live to see his estimates converted into the life policies we now know. Now anyone can choose between:

● A *term policy*, which is a type of insurance policy that provides for an agreed sum of money to be paid to the policyholder's family or next of kin but only if the policyholder happens to die within an agreed period of time;

● A *whole life policy*, which provides for an agreed sum of money

29

to be paid to the policyholder's family or next of kin when the policyholder dies, whenever that may be;
- An *endowment* policy, which provides a sum of money either at the end of an agreed period of time, or on the death of the policyholder, whichever of the two happens first; and
- An *annuity*, which is a form of life assurance that, like a pension, provides for a sum of money to be paid at regular intervals to the policyholder.

Lloyd's

Lloyd's is unique. It is not an insurance company. There is no equivalent of this remarkable insurance market to be found anywhere else in the world.

Since 1688, when Edward Lloyd first opened his coffee house in Tower Street for merchants to conduct their business, which often included underwriting of marine insurance risks, his successors (now known as the Corporation of Lloyd's) have fulfilled a similar function: the provision of a market-place for insurance. Lloyd's, of course, is no longer an informal assembly of merchants meeting in a coffee house.

Lloyd's today is a formally constituted Society of underwriters which comprise traditional "Names"—private individuals who trade with unlimited liability—and corporate members who trade with limited liability. The capital they provide supports 139 syndicates, which vary in size. Syndicates are managed by an underwriting agent who appoints a professional underwriter for each main class of business the syndicate deals with.

We shall be discussing the role of insurance brokers shortly, but in order to see how Lloyd's works, we need to begin with a Lloyd's broker bringing insurance business from a member of the public to Lloyd's. Let us assume it is a shipowner wishing to insure a new vessel.

The broker acting on behalf of the shipowner will immediately fill out a "slip", setting out the details of the risk involved, and take it to the Underwriting Room at Lloyd's. He will then approach the underwriters, sitting in the narrow boxes, who deal in marine business, seeking the best "quote" on behalf of the shipowner.

Once he has negotiated an acceptable rate, he gets the chosen underwriter to indicate on the slip what share of the total risk he is willing to accept. He is in effect "leading" the underwriting, and the broker then proceeds to get similar agreements from other underwriters on the same basis. In this way the risk is spread among several underwriters.

We have spoken of the capital standing behind the syndicates at Lloyd's. Each individual member—or Name—has to demonstrate an individual show of wealth to the Council of Lloyd's of at least £250,000. Names also have to lodge substantial funds at Lloyd's in proportion to the amount of business they can transact. Corporate members of Lloyd's are specially-formed companies which must have a minimum of £1.5 million of assets and entrust these to Lloyd's, much as an individual member does. All these funds are backed by the Lloyd's Central Fund, which stands in if a member cannot pay insurance claims and thus protects the policyholder.

In the late 1980s and early 1990s, Lloyd's suffered a series of losses of enormous proportion. In total over £7 billion had to be paid by its members, many of whom then sued their underwriting agents alleging that their affairs had been handled negligently. Cases of fraud had also been alleged earlier. The crisis which all this provoked in the market led to sweeping reforms. The main one was the introduction of limited liability capital (that is, from corporate members). As well as this break with tradition, Lloyd's overhauled virtually every aspect of the way in which it conducted business. These reforms began in earnest with the publication of Lloyd's first central business plan in April 1993. This ushered in a far more direct and centralised management style, to ensure the market's survival and that the mistakes of the past could not be repeated.

Lloyd's emerged from loss in 1993 when healthy profits returned to the market. Lloyd's still attracts business from around the world and in 1999 had an annual premium income capacity of £10 billion. The scope of Lloyd's market now extends well beyond its original marine business to include aviation, space technology, road transport, offshore oil and gas exploration and such marginal oddities as a comedian's moustache, a film star's legs, and insurance to cover the payment of large prizes—say for the capture of the Loch Ness Monster or perhaps a professional golfer's hole-in-one.

Insurance Brokers

We have concentrated so far on how the insurance market works and what kind of a service the insurance market, made up of insurance companies and Lloyd's, offers the public. In the case of Lloyd's, we made the point that authorised brokers were an essential link between the public and the Lloyd's underwriter.

General insurance and life business, both outside Lloyd's, are sold in several different ways. The companies and the life offices have branches up and down the country through which policies are sold

Where Insurance Firms Invest their Money (1997)

Long-term funds
£719,080m

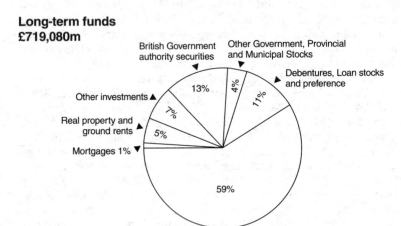

British Government authority securities

Other Government, Provincial and Municipal Stocks

Debentures, Loan stocks and preference

Other investments

Real property and ground rents

Mortgages 1%

13% 4% 11% 7% 5%

59%

Oridinary Stocks and Shares

General funds
£97,965m

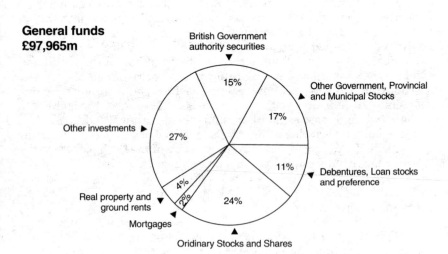

British Government authority securities

Other Government, Provincial and Municipal Stocks

Other investments

Real property and ground rents

Mortgages

Debentures, Loan stocks and preference

15% 17% 27% 11% 4% 2% 24%

Oridinary Stocks and Shares

The insurance companies covered include British firms and their overseas subsidiaries and British subsidiaries of overseas companies. The investments are at market value.

Source: Association of British Insurers

direct to the public. In addition, part-time agents, such as bank managers and solicitors, are often appointed by companies to channel business to them.

In addition there are the professional insurance brokers, who range from a small shop in the high street to a London-based international broker. They are full time specialists, offering detailed advice to clients, normally free of charge, receiving their income from a commission paid by the insurance companies (or Lloyd's underwriters). Such brokers offer independent advice not tied to one insurance company. At one time, it was easy to set up as an insurance broker. But since 1981, although firms can still set up as insurance intermediaries, a firm offering broking services has to be registered and to meet the stringent requirements of the Insurance Brokers Registration Act. At present some 15,400 individual insurance brokers have been registered. Some 2,500 businesses are entitled to trade as insurance brokers.

Foreign Business

Overseas business has been a significant part of the London insurance market for centuries. It remains so today. Over half of the total premiums flowing to Lloyd's and to the companies come from overseas. Only Switzerland can claim a higher figure.

This foreign business emerges in two ways—through the branches, agencies and subsidiaries of the companies in over 100 separate countries and through the insurance brokers who place the business with the companies or Lloyd's in London.

Something like a half of all the overseas business flowing to the London market comes from the United States, with a smaller share coming from members of the European Community.

The capacity of the London market is such that it can attract a larger share of the premiums arising from insurance business round the world than any other centre. It has enabled Lloyd's underwriters, for example, not only to pay out £150 million against claims when two earth satellites were lost in space, but also to finance their rescue by the space shuttle *Discovery*.

When such claims are deducted from the world-wide premiums, the London insurance market's net foreign income (*i.e.* its invisible income, which also includes portfolio income) comes out at £4,076 million. Further details are shown in Chapter 15.

Contribution to the Economy

We have now identified several ways in which the insurance companies and Lloyd's help the functioning of the economy and the smooth running, and expansion, of industry:

(i) By providing financial protection against loss from fire, theft, legal liability, pecuniary loss, interruption of production, etc., insurance companies ensure that such calamities are immediately paid for, enabling finance to be devoted to the development of business.

(ii) By accumulating funds, out of premiums, to pay out future claims, insurance companies are able to invest large sums not only in Government securities but in industry itself. At the end of 1999, investments by insurance companies in British Government securities, debentures, loan stocks, preference and guaranteed stocks and shares and ordinary stocks and shares were £817,000 million. We shall be examining how this happens in Chapter 5.

(iii) The insurance industry is a major employer, with the London market alone employing a workforce of some 40,000.

(iv) Close to 80 per cent of all households have an involvement in the insurance industry through life insurance and virtually all households have one or more general insurance policies.

(v) After the payment of claims from its world-wide premiums, the London insurance market's net foreign income (its invisible income including portfolio income) comes out at £7,417 million.

4. The Stock Exchange

What it Does

The London Stock Exchange remains at the centre of the City and a stock market is at the heart of capitalism.

In essence, it is the place where investors with money to spare make contact with those in industry, commerce and Government who want to borrow it. In fact it is a market in stocks and shares, that is, where pieces of paper representing the ownership of companies or loans to Government and others can be bought and sold.

A capitalist society can flourish without a stock market. But it is only when one exists that the cost of finding new money for enterprises declines and money begins to flow freely into them.

The fear that an investor cannot freely sell his shares in a company immediately blocks new financing. And the knowledge that an investment in a company (through the acquisition of shares) can be sold whenever it is needed elsewhere is a major incentive to investors. A stock market provides such re-assurance.

What it Is

Over close on the two centuries since its beginning, the Stock Exchange has had to adapt itself to the needs of investors and borrowers alike. Its constitution has also had to reflect these changes.

The original Deed of Settlement, which established the Stock Exchange in 1802, was revised in 1875 and, following fundamental changes (so-called "Big Bang") in 1986, under the Financial Services Act, was eventually exchanged for a new Memorandum and Articles of Association. This was when the Stock Exchange became a private, limited company. Five years later the Court of the Stock Exchange was replaced by a Board of Directors. We shall be explaining in a moment why such changes were necessary.

The present London Stock Exchange can now be said to be offering these services:

- It provides a market place for shares to be bought and sold and for new share issues to be offered;
- It is responsible for vetting companies before their shares can be listed and traded on the Exchange;
- It ensures that the Exchange works efficiently fairly by policing the market's mechanism;
- It vets new applicants for membership and ensures that existing members comply with its rules.

It is itself, a recognised investment exchange (RIE) regulated by the Financial Services Authority (see Chapter 16).

How it Began

Seventeenth century London was one of the largest trading ports in Europe and a centre for all kinds of economic activity. As the rewards of trade with the newly discovered continents increased, so did the risks, and many merchants were happier to take a part or a share of the venture, in return for a slice of the potential profits.

However, voyages were long and most investors were not prepared to put up money in the first place, unless they could cash in their shares whenever they wanted. This demand for liquidity led to holders of shares meeting at known places, often coffee-houses, where shares could be exchanged, or sold, and where entrepreneurs could go to find funds to finance their projects. Such meetings were taking place as early as the 1770s.

Not until 1802 was the Stock Exchange formally constituted, when it was felt necessary that a controlled and recognised procedure should be established to enable investors to buy and sell shares without undue difficulty or risk, and thus make it easier for companies to raise funds to finance expansion. This experience was not unique to London either; Amsterdam was the first city to develop such an Exchange and a host of capitalist countries have each felt a need to establish their own Exchanges at a particular stage in their economic development.

How it Used to Work

The easiest way to appreciate the way in which the actual workings of the London market have changed over the past decade or more is to consider an individual transaction. Let us assume that you have just inherited some money from a relative. You are advised by a stockbroker to invest some of the money on the Stock Exchange. Before the changes which took place in 1986, the stockbroker would act solely as a "middle man" between yourself, the client, and the wholesaler of shares known as the stockjobber.

The stockbroker had access to a lot of detailed information about the companies which are listed on the Exchange and would give you advice on which of these he recommended as a good investment. Having made your choice, aided by your stockbroker's professional opinion, he would then go onto the floor of the Exchange on your behalf and purchase the shares from a stockjobber. Members of the public were not allowed to buy shares from the jobbers directly. All transactions had to be carried out through the offices of a stockbroker. Once on the floor, the stockbroker would go round the various stalls, or jobbers' *"pitches"* as they were known, and ask the jobbers what was their price for the shares he wanted to buy. The broker would not say at that stage whether he was buying or selling, as the two prices (lower for buying, higher for selling) quoted to him by the jobbers would vary from pitch to pitch. Having worked out which jobber was selling at the cheapest, he could go back to him and arrange to purchase the shares on behalf of his client. Exactly the same process was gone through when a broker wished to sell shares on behalf of his client. It should be added that telephones and information screens also played their part in these transactions.

What we have described is the way in which the London market operated between 1908 and 1986. Under this arrangement, known as "single-capacity" dealing, the broker and the jobber had separate functions: the jobber acting as a wholesaler and making his profit from the margin between his buying and selling prices and from his dealings in the shares, the broker charging a fixed commission to his client. The jobber, having quoted a price, was obliged to trade with the broker, just as the broker was obliged to get the best possible price for his client.

Reasons for Change

This system worked well and not only protected the investor from a smart dealer wanting to off-load a block of doubtful shares, but ensured competitive prices from the jobbers, as well as smoothing out excessive price fluctuations.

On October 27, 1986, the Stock Exchange introduced major changes: the abolition of the fixed brokers' commission, the introduction of negotiated commissions and the end of "single capacity" dealings. The changes which took place are commonly referred to as "Big

Bang". Before these changes, preparations for 100 per cent ownership of dealing firms by other financial institutions had been completed. What we need to explore is why.

Several factors, some domestic, some international, had brought about this transformation. They were:

● The British Government's conviction that fixed commissions had been inhibiting competition in the London stock market.
● The dramatic rise in the volume of investing funds in the hands of big financial institutions, such as pension funds, insurance companies, unit and investment trusts, had put pressure on the fixed commission arrangements, and led to proposals for negotiated commissions.
● The financial cost of holding a growing volume of equity and fixed interest securities had strained the wholesale capacity of the jobbers and highlighted the lack of capital funds under present arrangements.
● A growing amount of London-based international security business had been by-passing the London Stock Exchange (because of the fixed commissions) and was being undertaken by the London offices of overseas security houses).
● Shares in certain major U.K. companies, such as ICI, had been trading more heavily in New York than in London.
● The growing international use of technology in security markets for information, communication and even dealing.

These were the main elements leading to the changes in 1986.

How it Works now

The process of change began on July 27, 1983, when the Chairman of the Stock Exchange agreed to abolish minimum commissions by the end of 1986. From this commitment emerged other structural changes.

The first was the proposal to change from "single capacity" to "dual capacity", under which a single firm can act both as agent and principal, acting on its own behalf as well as on behalf of its clients. This change in turn allowed (with the encouragement of the Stock Exchange and the Bank of England) individual firms to increase their capital resources and other financial institutions, such as banks, to buy stakes in such Member Firms. A dramatic change in the structure of the securities industry thus took place, with U.K. clearing and merchant banks and foreign banks acquiring stakes in existing broking and jobbing firms.

What emerged, therefore, on October 27, 1986 was a stock market whose members were composed of broker/dealers, market makers and retail service providers. At one end of this spectrum, market makers are capable of acting on behalf of clients as agents, of taking positions in shares, of making markets in shares, of assuming distribution and of undertaking their own research. At the other end brokers and retail service providers will look after the modest investment needs of you and me. Some of these dealers confine themselves to offering a "no frills" service, simply buying and selling shares on behalf of clients.

The new structure, which has been operational for a decade and a half, has enabled banks and investment houses to link with market makers, thus forming large financial conglomerates capable of competing with the giants of New York and Tokyo. These large groupings, backed by extensive financial resources, now combine the functions of issuing houses, market-makers, brokers, investment managers, deposit takers, providers of short and medium credit facilities, as well as insurance services.

The process of buying and selling shares reflects all this. An investor approaching a broker/dealer, wishing to buy, say, 1,500 shares in ICI, now relies, not on the competition between jobbers, as in the old days, but rather on the competitive prices offered and shown on individual screens. At first, when this system was introduced in 1986, prices were displayed on information screens on the floor of the Stock Exchange. But it was not long before the screens in broker/dealers' offices began to dominate operations and the floor eventually became redundant. Thus the market is now made up of computerised screens in brokers' offices linked together. Such technology has also changed and improved and is still doing so, as we shall see.

At present, as we enter the new Millennium, a private investor will still go to his broker to place his investment order or to seek advice, or both. What happens then depends on whether the broker deals through what is known as the "order book" or deals away from the "order book".

At first, market makers were obliged to display their bid and offer prices for all individual stocks, along with the maximum transaction size to which these prices related. Such prices were firm so far as other members were concerned. Prices for larger transactions were subject to negotiation. Thus market makers competed to make the best quote. In essence it was (and still is, in areas where the system still operates) a "quote-driven" system and was supported by the Stock Exchange Automated Quotations (SEAQ) service, a continuously up-dated database providing market makers' bids and offers digitally to the market. This quote-driven system applied to *all* transactions until a new round of technology was introduced, and it still applies to small orders and for shares outside the FTSE 100 index. Where it does not apply is in the area where improved technology has been applied, *i.e.* through the Stock Exchange Electronic Trading System (SETS) which is being used for trading the top industrial shares. Begun in October, 1997, this has introduced automated trading to the shares in the FTSE 100 index, that is, to the top 100 shares. It is called "the order book".

Under it, when bid and offer prices for any of the top 100 shares match, orders are automatically executed against each other on the screen—with increased speed and efficiency. Investors deal through their broker directly or through a special retail service provider (who is also a member of the Exchange), and they in turn display their bid (buying) and offer (selling) orders to the market on the screen, what is in effect an electronic order book.

One further point needs an explanation: the nature of the orders given by investors to their broker in relation to shares in the FTSE 100 index. There are in fact four different kinds of orders which are not hard to understand:

Limit   This specifies the size and price at which an investor wishes to deal. If it is matched the order is executed immediately. If not, it remains on the "order book".

Fill or kill   These orders are either executed immediately in full or rejected.

At best   Buy or sell orders are entered and executed immediately at the best price available.

Execute and eliminate   Similar to "at best" but with a specified limit price so that it is matched immediately at no worse than the specified price.

Experience of the "order-driven" system in other markets abroad has shown that it improves efficiency and leads to a lowering of the costs of trading. This has been London's experience too. The margin (known as "the spread") between the buying and selling price has narrowed, turnover has increased and market liquidity improved. The London Stock Exchange hopes to extend the range of the "order book" (*i.e.* SETS) to include the next 250 companies, thus attracting further business to London.

Who Owns Shares

Share ownership has risen significantly in recent years. The latest survey, carried out at the end of 1998 by MORI Finance Services, on behalf of ProShare and the London Stock Exchange showed that there are currently 12 million people in the U.K. (27 per cent of the adult population) who own shares. This compared with an estimated 9 per cent in 1979. Only Sweden (around 50%), the U.S. (40%), Denmark (33%) and Australia (32%) have higher percentages.

Several factors have helped this trend:

● The tax incentives offered to *employee share schemes*. In 1979 there were only 30 such schemes. Now there are 5,829 covering both all-employee share schemes and discretionary ones for executives.

● The Government's *privatisation programme* boosted personal share ownership. By returning close on 50 state-owned companies to the free enterprise sector (including British Gas, British Aerospace, Britoil, the Electricity industry, water companies, TSB, British Airways and British Telecom), individuals who had not previously considered stock market investment became shareholders for the first time.

● The introduction of *personal equity plans* (PEPs). Over 15.5 million and 4.5 million have been taken out since 1987.

Sources: ProShare (U.K.); London Stock Exchange

How CREST settles business

In the global securities market that is emerging it is necessary to provide a way of settling the payment for stocks and shares that is not only convenient to investors but also competitive with other centres. To prevent London falling behind other centres it became imperative for a new system to be devised quickly. The outcome was a Bank of England initiative which swiftly led to two inter-linked decisions: to move from fixed settlement days to rolling settlements and to design and introduce a new system to be known as CREST.

The rolling settlements began with a ten-day cycle in July 1994 and then moved to a five-day cycle. The aim of the system is to reduce costs, by taking much of the paperwork out of the system, to reduce

risk by shortening the settlement period and to provide a high standard of exchange (delivery against payments).

CREST works as follows. It in effect responds to electronic messages
from members to transfer stock between accounts. It then authentic-
ates the messages and compares the instructions given by both buyer
and seller and matches them. On settlement day it checks the availab-
ility of stock and cash in the CREST members' accounts and moves
stock from the seller's account to the buyer's. The buying member's
account is instructed to pay the member's bank and is unconditionally
obliged to do so. The system also notifies the stock's registrar who
registers valid transfers within two hours of the electronic transfer.

New safeguards

The emergence under the present system of new, enlarged financial
supermarkets has brought anxieties as well as opportunities. There
are the obvious dangers of conflicts of interest within the same firm.
There is also the danger that clients may suffer from the ability of a
firm to act as both agent and as principal.

In other words, a broker/dealer might be tempted to recommend
shares to a client which he has acquired as a principal. He may also
be tempted to use information acquired in one capacity in executing
a different. As the City jargon put it, the gaps in the "Chinese walls"
erected between one activity and another could lead to rather too
much temptation.

Safeguards have clearly been needed. To understand what form
these new safeguards take, let us first of all see how the investor is
still protected under dual capacity.

Going back to our original client with a sum of money to invest, we
must remember that under the old system no matter which broker he
chose to do business with, the broker's commission on the deal was
fixed. Therefore, brokers could not undercut each other, and similarly
when on the floor of the Exchange, all brokers were obliged to find
the best deal they could for their client. This being so, the broker had
nothing to gain by suggesting poorly performing shares to his client;
as his commission was secure, he offered the best advice he could,
and found shares at the best price.

Also under the old single-capacity system, we remember that jobbers were not allowed to deal with the public directly. They only
bought or sold when a broker wished to sell or buy from them and
in this way investors could never be sold poorly performing shares
unwittingly, since the broker was always there to act as advisor and

professional go-between, with the client on one side and the jobber on the other.

However, under the present system of dual-capacity dealings, one can easily see how, if a dealer in shares is left with a particularly poor portfolio, he can say to a prospective client, "I recommend you to buy share X, and I just happen to have 5,000 of them which I will be pleased to sell you".

Under the former system of single capacity this could never arise, as the broker would know that share X was a bad buy and would dissuade his client from investing in it. Similarly, it might be asked, what is to stop a dealer buying shares from a client at below the market price or selling him a particular share above the odds? Again, under single-capacity dealing, the broker was duty bound to get the best price.

Since the introduction of dual capacity in 1986, therefore, additional safeguards have been needed:

● The introduction of the Financial Services Act provided a statutory frame-work covering investor protection, ensuring all securities houses undertaking investment business on behalf of clients complied with the rules laid down in the Act.

● Under the Exchange's computerised systems and SEAQ (Stock Exchange Automated Quotations System) and SETS (Stock Exchange Electronic Trading System) the dissemination of price information has become more visible to investors and market practitioners than ever before.

● A comprehensive set of conduct of business rules, which govern the relationship between the client and member firm or securities house, ensure that clients are made aware of the firm's terms of dealing and in turn that firms put the interests of clients ahead of their own at all times. All registered securities houses are therefore required to abide by these rules.

In addition the Stock Exchange has extensive systems for supervising and monitoring the dealings of firms in each of its markets and for enforcing compliance with the rules governing member firms' activities.

The Exchange has direct access to the information input by firms into the central Checking System and the central price display mechanisms, SEAQ, SEAQ International and SETS. This coupled with the information provided to the Exchange's Regulatory News Service, allows the Exchange to maintain a comprehensive database of detailed information which can be used to investigate any irregularities. In addition, the Exchange's Market Regulation and Enforcement Department co-operates closely with the FSA.

The Exchange's stringent rules regulating its membership, together with close scrutiny and monitoring of the Exchange's markets, should ensure investor confidence, thus rendering the London Stock Exchange a safe and secure market in which to trade.

5. The Capital Market

Money can be provided to an industrial firm in the form of a credit (see Chapter 2) or in the form of an issue of shares, debentures, bonds, etc. (see Chapter 4). The banks and the stock market are the dual providers. In one case money is lent to a borrower; in the other a financial instrument is bought and sold.

Some financial centres, for historical reasons, rely basically on bank finance; others on a combination of bank finance and stock market securities.

Active capital markets, like London and New York, can provide a variety of financial sources. Increasingly, they are also offering "derivative" products such as options, futures, etc. (see Chapter 13). The key to a successful centre is the provision of new money and this in turn depends not only on flexible bank finance, but also on the existence of financial instruments and of financial institutions capable of absorbing a growing volume of new securities. London's capital market is made up of:

(i) A stock market providing a *primary* market in new securities and a *secondary* market in existing securities.
(ii) Financial institutions, such as insurance companies, pension funds, investment trusts and unit trusts.
(iii) Specialised financial institutions, such as Investors in Industry, Equity Capital for Industry, Commonwealth Development Finance Company and the Agricultural Mortgage Corporation.
(iv) A wide range of derivative instruments.

The size of funds available for investment through the main institutions (insurance companies, pension funds, investment trusts and unit trusts) can be judged from the following table:

Total assets (end March 1998)	(£ billions)
Insurance companies:	
Long-term funds	719.1
General funds	97.9
Pension funds	617.0
Investment trusts	61.0
Unit trusts	183.6

The way in which insurance companies and life offices accumulate their funds was explained in Chapter 3. We now need to look more closely into pension funds, investment trusts and unit trusts.

A. Pension Funds

What they Are   Pension funds arise out of the efforts to provide pensions (*i.e.* regular agreed payments) to employed people after they have retired. Some pension schemes, such as those relating to the central Civil Service, are financed direct from the Exchequer; that is, the ultimate pensions really come out of current tax revenue. But the bulk of occupational pension schemes are based on the pooling of regular payments into a trust fund, out of which future pensions will be paid.

A young person in his first job can, if he remains in employment, expect to be receiving wages or salaries for the next 45 or even 50 years and, thereafter, a pension for the rest of his life. His, and his employers', contributions to the pension fund are thus piling up for a lengthy period before the retirement payments become due.

The pooling of the contributions, therefore, is the source for investments on the stock market and elsewhere. These investments have to match the pension funds' long-term obligations, which in spite of the growing portability of pensions, can cover the need to pay out retirement pensions up to 40 or even 45 years ahead.

How they Invest   The way in which pension funds make investments vary, though the underlying obligations are clear. Pension funds are basically trust funds and as such the trustees are bound by legal restraints, imposed by their own trust deed and trust law. The trustees in turn will normally take investment advice from a bank, an insurance company or other professional investment adviser or, of the fund is big enough, from an in-house investment manager.

Their approach to investment is based on a number of factors: the

Fund Management in the City

Investors, large and small, domestic and foreign seek advice in the City. They have been doing so for centuries. But the scale of such advice and investment has only recently become fully realised. Funds worth well over £2,000 billion are now actively managed in the U.K. Of the total over £500 billion is on behalf of overseas clients. Several features stand out:

- In real terms the value of U.K. institutional client funds have increased fourfold since 1980.
- Assets invested in insurance and pension funds account for the bulk of the U.K. institutional funds, although unit trust funds have become more important and should attract more European funds now that OIEC's in a familiar form are available (see this Chapter).
- Management is undertaken by the large insurance companies (38%), investment/merchant banks (38%), independent firms (16%) and self-managed pension funds (8%). The top ten companies account for a quarter of the total.
- The bulk of the management in the U.K. is naturally done in London, but the role of Edinburgh too needs to be emphasised (see table below). In terms of institutional equity management London is now top of the world league table:

Top International Centres
(\$ billions)

City	1997	1996	1995
1. London	1,807	1,218	1,016
2. New York	1,552	1,125	896
3. Boston	1,128	826	603
4. Tokyo	1,104	1,638	1,524
5. Zurich	579	423	411
6. San Francisco	478	361	289
7. Los Angeles	365	292	242
8. Paris	338	289	261
9. Frankfurt	251	169	157
14. Edinburgh	188	167	137

age of the fund, the blend of ages of the employees, and their view of economic and financial trends, stretching decades ahead.

The age of the fund inevitably affects its rate of growth, since in the early years the income from contributions and from investments outstrips the outflow of retirement pensions. It normally takes some considerable time for a fund to reach a static position, that is, where its income and outgoings offset each other. Few British funds have yet reached this position, except in declining industries such as merchant shipping and coal.

Most factors point to the need for a long-term policy: the need to consider the future pension requirements of the latest recruit will itself stretch the investment horizon at least 60 years ahead. In a normal, still growing scheme, the investment advisers will be looking 40 or more years ahead.

How will this affect their choice of investments? A few general points will illustrate how they tend to go about it:

(i) They will want to ensure a guaranteed income flow for a long-ish period. This may point to the acquisition of long-dated Government securities.

(ii) They will want to ensure capital growth in the fund's assets. This may suggest investments in industrial ordinary shares (equities).

(iii) They will be aware of the dangers of future inflation. This too may tempt them to consider ordinary shares and index-linked Government bonds.

(iv) They will be aware that longer-term obligations enable them to await certain investment developments. They can, therefore, consider investing in large-scale developments, where income is delayed.

(v) They will be aware of having future obligations in sterling, but conscious of obtaining a better chance of growth in equity markets overseas. Often this may suggest a target of over 20 per cent of foreign equities.

These are just a few of the factors to be considered in deciding on the final blend of their investments. Their decisions will then make up part of the total institutional investments on the stock market and elsewhere. The pension funds have become a powerful influence on the capital market over the past decade and a half. Two have assets of over £20 billion. Seven have assets of over £10 billion. Their total assets are now some £617 billion.

The Largest U.K. Pension Funds

Market Value of Investment Funds, 1998

	£ billions
British Coal	22.9
British Telecom	22.7
Electricity Supply	18.8
Universities	17.2
Post Office	15.0
British Gas	12.9
Railways	12.7
Lloyds TSB	10.3
Barclays Bank	10.0
British Petroleum	9.5
British Airways	8.9
Shell	8.4
British Steel	8.3
National Westminster Bank	7.9
ICI	6.6
BBC	6.0
Stanhope	5.8
Greater Manchester	5.4
Midland Bank	5.2

(Source: National Association of Pension Funds Year Book 1999)

B. Investment Trusts

Spreading risks seems to be a City habit. It is, as we have already seen, the basis of insurance. It is also the investment approach taken by both investment trusts and unit trusts.

Both kinds of trusts approach the investment issue (and its solution) differently: but both work on the principle of *not* having all your eggs in the same basket. They provide a method whereby a non-professional investor can invest small amounts of money in a variety of shares. The easiest way to understand how they do this is to explain how each works and then to compare one with the other.

How Investment Trusts Started   Investment trusts were on the scene first, roughly half a century before unit trusts. The Foreign and Colonial Government Trust, formed in 1868 and quoted on the Stock Exchange just over ten years later, invested in a selection of eighteen overseas government stocks. The aim then, and now, was to give the investor of moderate means the same advantage as the large investor in reducing his risk by spreading the investment over a number of different stocks, so that the risk would be spread and the individual investor would not be in a position of losing all his savings if one of the shares chosen suddenly collapsed. Even the spreading of risks did not save some of the early participants, especially during the so-called Baring Crisis of 1890. But other investment trusts, including the Foreign and Colonial Government Trust, survived and lessons were learnt.

Buying Investment Trust Shares A decade ago, the only way to buy shares in an investment trust was through a stockbroker or dealer, as for any other shares. Now, however, managers of investment trusts have introduced savings schemes and investment schemes, which are a way to buy shares directly through the managers, often at less cost than going to a dealer in shares. They can also be bought in the form of Personal Equity Plans or from share dealing services such as Charles Schwab.

How They Work An investment trust is a company, quoted on the Stock Exchange, which invests shareholders' funds, not in machinery to make things, but in shares in other companies. The choice of shares is made by professional investment trust managers. The income from the shares chosen is largely distributed to its own shareholders by way of dividend and partly used to cover its running costs and to build up reserves for lean years. Most investment trusts aim at high capital appreciation for their stockholders, reflected in the price of the shares and underlying asset values.

This process gives the investment trust several features:

(i) It spreads the investment risks over several shares.
(ii) It can provide exposure to overseas markets, special situations, unlisted securities etc.
(iii) It provides professional investment expertise.
(iv) Dividend income is distributed regularly among the investment trust's shareholders and the price of the investment trust share in the stock market, together with its asset value, reflects some of the success (or failure) of the investment policy used.

How "Gearing" Works One additional investment trust feature arises from the relationship between a trust's ordinary shareholders and its ability to borrow further funds to purchase additional shares. This kind of borrowing is a form of "gearing" (or "leverage" in the

United States). In simple terms, such borrowing, through a term loan, for example, enables a trust to buy more shares. If the stock market rises, there is capital appreciation, which enables the trust to service the loan. If share prices fall, the reverse happens.

On this basis, the ordinary shareholder will receive a dividend related to the success or failure of the investments (after the term loan interest has been paid). Now when the stock market is rising and an investment trust's investments are sharing in its buoyancy, a trust's ordinary shareholders will be receiving a higher proportion of its total income than their nominal share and the reverse will be true when the stock market is falling. This so-called "gearing" means that the whole of the growth in income, over and above the servicing of the loan, accrues to the ordinary shareholder. It explains why shares of investment trusts with high gearing (*i.e.* a high proportion of borrowing) will rise faster than the Stock Exchange average when share prices are rising and will fall faster than the average when the stock market is falling. Borrowing can also take place abroad, but in this case the trust has also to contend with fluctuations in the value of a loan expressed in foreign currency.

You may wonder what happens when stock markets fall, as they occasionally do. Fortunately, there are ways of protecting shareholders from the *adverse* effects of "gearing". One of the most common is for the investment manager to "go liquid", that is, to arrange to sell certain shares and hold the money in cash. Secondly, he can invest a proportion of his total fund in loan capital or preference shares. Thirdly, he could consider buying back the trust's own loan capital. Each method has the effect of protecting the trust's ordinary shareholder from a bigger than normal drop in his income. The difficulty, of course, lies in guessing when such protection is needed.

Why There is a Discount The fixed capital of an investment trust can be switched from one share to another. This flexibility is helped by the Inland Revenue agreement not to charge them tax on any capital gains. Such gains are not distributed in cash, but are used to build up the investment trust's portfolio. Basically a trust's assets are increased, when it invests successfully.

The valuation of a trust's assets thus becomes a major measuring rod of a trust's success. Net asset values (that is gross assets less liabilities) can then be compared with a trust's share valuation. If a trust's net assets are divided by the number of a trust's ordinary shares, the result is what is known as "net asset per share" and can be compared with the share price of the trust in the stock market. If the share price is above the net asset value per share, it is said to stand at a *premium*; if below, it is said to be at a *discount*.

What accounts for the discount? The answer is a combination of factors. To some extent it reflects the cost of breaking up an investment trust to get at the basic shares; to some extent it reflects the competition from other, more publicised, investment vehicles, such as unit trusts; and to some extent it reflects the share performance of individual trusts. Whatever the reason, the discount means that such an investment is costing the shareholder in an investment trust less than if he invested directly in the underlying shares.

The original aim of the first investment trusts, apart from spreading risks, was to secure a high income for its shareholders. Some still concentrate on income. But specialisation now has spread to other targets, such as capital growth or overseas investment, or individual industries. In addition there are now so-called "Split Capital Trusts" whose shares are divided into income shares, capital shares, zero dividend preference shares and stepped preference shares, giving holders a choice. The variety is remarkable. There are now over 300 investment trusts, split into some 20 different categories, managing some £61 billion of investors' funds with the spread of specialisation covering most geographical areas and industry sectors.

C. Unit Trusts

How Unit Trusts Started   Unit trusts are more recent arrivals on the City scene. They can be said to have begun in 1931 when a London stockbroker brought the idea with him from a visit to the United States. As a result Municipal and General launched the First British Fixed Trust on April 22, 1931.

The original idea was that investors' money would be invested in a *fixed* number of chosen shares, which would be held for an agreed number of years. This would ensure a spreading of the risks and a higher yield than was obtainable on 2.5 per cent Consols. The experiment was successful, various flexibilities were introduced and by 1939 there were no less than 89 such unit trusts, operated by 15 management companies, with some £80 million under investment.

How they Work   The best way to understand how unit trusts work is to compare them with the investment trusts we have just been considering. The basic difference is that, whereas supply and demand for investment trust shares affect the share price of the trust itself, demand for unit trusts simply affects the size of the fund. The price of unit trusts, which is usually calculated daily, depends on the value of the underlying assets. Unit trusts are thus said to be "open-ended";

that is, they can grow or shrink and their size depends entirely on the purchase or sale of units by investors.

Let's take this step by step. Money invested in a unit trust is pooled in a trust fund which invests the money in stocks and shares. Its deed is usually drawn up by the managers of the fund and the trustee, and authorised by the Financial Services Authority (FSA, see Chapter 16). The trustee is there to safeguard the fund, the management to undertake the investments and, with others, the sale of the units. A leading bank or insurance company normally acts as trustee. Thus the investor buys or sells "units" and the money is added or subtracted from the trust fund.

Unit trust prices are quoted in the newspapers showing a higher and a lower figure. The lower figure is now called the "sell" price and is the figure at which the managers are ready to buy back units from existing investors; the higher figure is the "buy" price at which they are prepared to sell new or existing units. The "buy" price includes the cost of buying the underlying securities together with the managers' initial charge, which is calculated by a formula laid down by the FSA.

Unit trusts can be attractive to small investors who have lump sums to invest and to those who wish to save on a regular basis. By spreading risks, they are a way of ensuring that you do not have all your eggs in one basket. They also offer a spectrum of different objectives: from "cash" or "money market" funds (for the short-term investor) to "equity" or "bond" funds (for the medium-term) and "equity" funds for the longer-term, say, over 7 years.

Unit trusts have come a long way since they were introduced into the U.K. in 1931. They have become much more flexible and specialised in the way they are managed and organised. They now offer a vehicle for the small and professional investor alike. They offer the advantage of spread of risks, professional management and access to funds on demand. They were naturally given a boost by the tax efficient Personal Equity Plans (PEP's) and, hopefully, should still benefit as these are replaced by Individual Savings Accounts (ISA's). Unit trusts are also an essential part of combined unit-linked packages with the life assurance industry. And, through various offshore financial centres, they offer a variety of so-called "off-shore units" (although these funds operate to different rules and are not always covered by compensation schemes).

At present approximately 1,600 different unit trusts are available and total investments at the last count had reached over £183 million.

New Vehicle   So far we have been using the word "trust" to describe the original fund vehicle designed to offer investors units of investment. Over the last two or three years, new investment companies, with a different corporate basis, have also been possible. These are known as OIEC's, short for "open-ended investment companies" and pronounced "oiks". By their introduction the industry has increasingly been enabled to offer its funds with a single price, instead of the dual pricing employed by trusts which we described earlier.

As companies, rather than trusts, OIEC's have their assets looked after by authorised depositories, usually a bank, instead of trustees. They also offer more flexibility. So far as the managers of funds are concerned the new vehicle makes it easier for them to house a set of funds under a single company and thus to rationalise the funds they have. As for investors, OIEC's make it easier to understand the pricing structure. For example, when needing to value shareholdings in an OIEC, investors simply multiply the number of shares held by the price shown. Charges too are more clearly set out. The sales charge is shown as a separate cost item, rather than being included in the bid/offer price. All this brings them into line with the practice elsewhere in Europe.

How the Different Funds Compare		
Unit Trusts	*OIEC's*	*Investment Trusts*
Under trust law	Company law	Company law
Investor buys units	Investor buys shares	Investor buys shares
Units can increase or decrease (open-ended)	Fund can increase or decrease (open-ended)	Fixed number of shares (closed ended)
Dual pricing (buy and sell prices)	Single pricing	Dual pricing (buy and sell prices)
Normally valued daily	Normally valued daily	Normally valued monthly
Limited ability to borrow	Limited ability to borrow	Ability to borrow (gearing/leverage)
Supervised by trustee	Supervised by depositary: optional independent directors	Stock Exchange requires independent directors

6. The Gilt-edged Market

What it is

As we noticed in Chapter 4, turnover in Government securities forms a substantial proportion of Stock Exchange business. The market in Government securities, otherwise known as the gilt-edged market (from the high-quality gilt-edged paper of the early certificates) is significant for other reasons too. At a time of high Government borrowing from the public, it becomes intertwined both with the Budget (fiscal policy) and interest rates (monetary policy). It deserves a chapter on its own.

How it began

Until recently the gilt-edged market was closely connected with the Bank of England and the Stock Exchange. One controlled it; the other used to house it. And it is not surprising to find that all three were just as closely intertwined at the beginning.

Kings and governments have needed to borrow throughout history. After centuries of such borrowings (and defaults) by kings of England and their governments, a more formal arrangement was agreed in 1694, when the British Government borrowed a further £1,200,000 to support the war against France, in return for the incorporation of the Bank of England, with the right to issue notes up to the value of its capital. Just over a century later, as we noted earlier, the Stock Exchange was formally established and, within a year, issued its first regular official list of prices. Gilt-edged stocks (though not described as such until 1892) were prominent in the list.

The Bank of England thus became the Government's agent in raising official loans and eventually the Stock Exchange became the obvious market place for their sale and purchase. For most of the eighteenth century, Government securities were sold to companies such as the East India Company and rich friends of ministers. Then, towards the end of the eighteenth century, Government stock was extended to the public generally.

However, from April 1998, the Bank's responsibility was transferred to the Treasury and the Debt Management Office (DMO) now makes all official operational decisions in the gilt-edged market.

Why it is Needed

The Bank of England still retains the role of central government cash management. It issues Treasury bills to the financial institutions; it holds the Government's main Exchequer accounts into which nearly all taxes and the proceeds of all official borrowings flow; and it keeps a record of all Government stockholders, makes all interest payments and arranges the final repayment or conversion of existing securities.

The Government issues its own securities to the public for a simple reason. In spending money on roads, schools, housing, hospitals, defence, etc., a Government will often incur expenditure beyond the inflow of taxes. Sometimes this will be seasonal, since tax bills fall due at certain times of the year. Sometimes it will be deliberate, in an attempt to stimulate the economy. Whatever the reason, the Government will need to borrow money from the public. And the DMO, as its agent, will arrange the issue of Government securities, ranging from three-months' Treasury bills to gilt-edged stocks with a maturity of thirty years or more. In undertaking this task between 1786 and 1986 the Bank of England used the senior partner of Mullens & Co. as the Government Broker.

What Gilts Are

The market on which such Government securities are bought and sold is now run by 16 gilt-edged market-makers. If you or I wish to buy Government securities, we have a choice. We can buy securities which have no final repayment date, referred to as "undated". In this case the price simply moves up and down in relation to current rates of interest. We can buy securities with repayment dates up to five years ahead known as "shorts"; from five to fifteen years ("medium"); or over fifteen ("longs"); in general, these are known as "conventionals". Some Government securities have been issued which are index-linked, that is, they allow for annual inflation and are directly linked to the retail price index. More recently a new type of security has been issued which has a "floating rate" of interest which is linked to the three month interest rate in the sterling money market.

Gilt-edged stocks have several characteristics. The main ones are that they are mainly fixed-interest debt instruments; the interest payments and eventual redemption (where appropriate) are obligations of Government; they usually have a redemption date (that is a date on which full repayment is made); and they have an interest rate "coupon", that is, the amount of interest to be paid each year (usually half-yearly) on the nominal value of the stock. Since the coupon rate per £100 of nominal stock is fixed (with the exception of the "floating rate gilt") when the stock is issued, change in the stock's market price leads to a corresponding change in its yield. For example, if £100 nominal of a 10 per cent stock is bought at a market price of £200, the running yield to the purchaser will be five per cent on the sum invested. Because of this connection, changes in the level of interest rates will be reflected in changes in the price of Government securities.

At present, gilt-edged stocks offer several advantages to the purchaser. The brokers' commission is much lower than on industrial shares. They do not attract stamp duty (although its imposition on equities will disappear soon). And, under current legislation, they do not become liable for capital gains tax.

How Gilts are Issued

Stocks are made available in two ways: by public offers and by what are known as "tap" sales to the market-makers. Offers are by auction.

Prospectuses for new issues are advertised in selected national newspapers, and application forms are also available from the DMO.

Large issues of conventional and index-linked stock are generally sold by auction. Professional investors state the price at which they are prepared to bid for stock (known as competitive bids). If the auction is oversubscribed, only the highest such bids will be successful.

Separate arrangements, however, are made for private investors who may apply (on a non-competitive basis) for a minimum of £1,000 and a maximum of £500,000 of stock (£250,000 for index-linked auctions) and they will receive stock at the average of the prices paid by successful competitive bidders. On this basis they do better than some of the professionals.

No commission is payable to the DMO on purchases of stock made through auctions.

The total value of Government stock outstanding at the end of March 1999 was some £262 billion.

Amount of Gilt-Edged Stocks

(£ millions)

End March	1997	1998	1999
Conventional	226,632	226,565	223,106
Index-Linked	28,952	31,902	32,602
Floating Rate	8,700	8,700	3,000
Undated	3,181	3,178	3,178
Total	267,465	270,345	261,886

Source: U.K. Debt Management Office

How the Market Works

The structure of the market changed radically after "Big Bang". In line with the changes introduced in the stock market generally, the gilt-edged market was also transformed. The introduction of dual capacity meant an end to the operations of the jobbing firms and the introduction of several new operators. The market now consists of three different participants:

- *Market-makers*. These are primary dealers, obliged to make an effective two-way market in gilts at all times and to accept DMO supervision. They deal direct with the big financial institutions by telephone.
- *Inter-dealer brokers*. They provide dealing facilities between the market-makers.
- *Broker dealers*. They provide agency facilities for investors, but also deal as principals if they so wish.

The gilt-edged market is still part of the Stock Exchange and the participants are members of the Stock Exchange and thus subject to its regulations, as well as being supervised by the DMO.

As in the case of the Stock Exchange generally, the gilt-edged market uses information screens, especially between the market-makers and the inter-dealer brokers who provide dealing facilities between them. Dissemination of prices is now by telephone or on screens.

The new technology has also extended to the *Central Gilts Office*, which offers a computerised service of payments and settlements

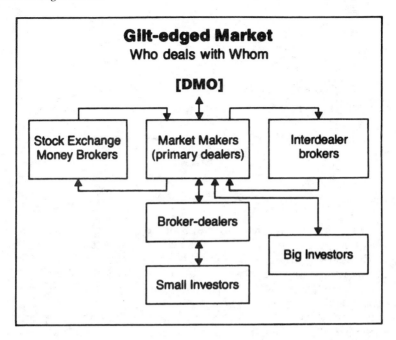

between members. This eliminates the need for paper transfers, certificates and cheques; it reduces settlement risks; and it is easy to use, enabling members to see their up-to-date stock positions at the touch of a button.

Thus the present gilt-edged market is now similar to the American pattern of primary dealers. One basic difference remains, however. The DMO has become part of the market with its own dealing room. Secondly, London maintains the distinction between gilt-edged dealers and the money market.

The method of selling new securities is evolving further, if only to ensure London competes with practices in New York and other centres. These innovations include the creation of a market in gilt "repos". This is short for a sale and "re-purchase agreement" and should allow investors to sell and buy back securities at a future date. The innovations also include tax changes and the introduction of what is known as a "strips facility", that is the ability to separate interest and principle payments for trading purposes.

7. The Money Market

What it does

When we were considering how banks make use of the deposits left with them, we said they had found it prudent to keep some of the money in cash or on short-term loan to the money market, just in case some of the depositors wanted their money back in a hurry. The short-term loans were said to be "liquid", that is they could be turned into cash quickly.

This leads us straight to the heart of the London money market and to the role it plays in the City. Its function is a simple one: to borrow and lend spare money for short periods. It is hardly the place you or I would invest the odd £50. But it is the equivalent of a savings deposit account for the big financial institutions, large industrial corporations, local authorities, even governments. And, hardly surprisingly, the British Government has found it useful for its own monetary purposes.

The Past

In the past the traditional money market was centred on the discount houses, which dealt in bills of exchange, certificates of deposit and other short-term instruments. They were specially capitalised, were largely financed by short-term borrowing from the banking system and given certain privileges by the Bank of England. In return they agreed to put in sufficient bids to cover the weekly Treasury bill tender.

In effect their role was to act as a monetary buffer between the banks and the Bank of England, channelling cash from the banks to other borrowers, both Government and commercial, through the purchase of bills, and short-term Government securities.

The discount houses and bill brokers played this role for more than a century and a half. During this period which extended into the 1970's, the so-called bill of exchange was the main borrowing instrument used. It was in effect evidence of a debt owed by one party to another, in respect of a trading transaction, and with an agreed date of payment, perhaps three months ahead. If the bill was simply drawn by one industrial firm and "accepted" by another—its trading counterpart—it would be called a "trade bill", but normally bills were accepted by a bank (an "accepting house") who undertook to become principally liable for payment at the bill's maturity. They then became known as "bank bills".

Originally the bill of exchange was used to finance the bulk of domestic trade by the large numbers of country banks. The bill brokers, the forerunners of the discount houses, made a market in these inland bills. As foreign trade developed, financed through London, the same mechanism was used and the international "bill on London" came into prominence.

It was at this stage that the merchant banks (or accepting houses) began to accept a growing volume of these bills, making them particularly attractive to the discount houses, who were keen to buy them below their ultimate repayment price (*i.e.* at a discount, which would depend on the prevailing rate of interest). The discount houses would "endorse" such bills, that is add their names, and therefore their guarantee, to the bills. Over the years other borrowing instruments were introduced too, especially Treasury bills and short-term Government securities, by which the Government borrows money from the financial institutions.

How it Operates Now

The traditional money market has been gradually replaced and widened over the past two decades, reflecting the abolition of exchange control, the liberalisation of markets generally and, more recently, the need to bring London practices into line with European central bank practices.

The wholesale money market is now made up of banks, commercial firms, local authorities, building societies and other financial institutions. The instruments used include inter-bank deposits, certificates of deposit, Treasury bills, local authority bills, eligible and ineligible bank bills, and sterling commercial paper. Short-term funds are lent between institutions either direct or through brokers, sometimes on an "unsecured" basis, *i.e.* not backed up with securities as collateral.

Although one sector of the market spills over into another, it is also a series of specialised markets. The specialisations cover lending to banks, local authorities, finance houses, etc. The markets operate through the placing and taking of short-term deposits and the purchase and sale of certificates of deposit, in sterling and foreign currencies.

The bulk of the business consists of inter-bank transactions and the market has now become the main means for the transformation of retail deposits into wholesale funds for bank lending of all kinds. It is also the basis of the Euro-dollar market, since it attracts foreign currency deposits as well as sterling.

To sum up, the money markets have the following characteristics:

- They link the major borrowers and lenders in short-term money together through money brokers.
- Their loans are unsecured.
- The Bank of England does not intervene directly in them.
- They provide the banks with a flexible source for funding their loans.
- They provide the mechanism for the transformation of maturities in the Euro-currency market.

Who Uses the Markets?

We have already indicated the variety of institutions which make use of the wholesale money market. They range from industrial and commercial firms to the leading financial institutions (banks, building societies, finance houses, etc.) and from local authorities to central Government.

The financial services to the City itself are self-evident. What are not so obvious are the services to industry.

The market's bill discounting facilities are familiar, stretching back into the nineteenth century. They can be highly competitive with the more normal lending techniques of overdrafts or fixed-term loans. But lending is not the only facility available to industry and commerce. Borrowing, especially for short periods, can be equally rewarding.

Commercial money can be left in the money market for varying periods and remain both secure and liquid. A variety of instruments and facilities are on offer. Cash can be deposited overnight, at call (that is available at 24 hours' notice) or for any fixed maturity the lender specifies. On substantial sums, a rate close to the inter-bank rate will normally be paid.

A growing number of industrial firms now have regular telephone links with money brokers and have already become part of the City's regular money business.

How Monetary Policy Works

We have mentioned several times that the Government uses the money market to transmit its influence on monetary policy to the rest of the economy. It is time to explain how.

Although the mechanism has been tampered with several times in recent years, the key to the transmission process lies with the Bank of England. It plays two crucial roles: it acts as banker to the Government; it also acts as banker to the banks. It is, therefore, directly involved in day-to-day transactions between the Government and the banks. Large sums of money flow from one to the other, through the Bank of England's accounts. The Bank can affect these flows through its operations in the money market.

This is not the place to explain monetary policy or even monetarism in any great detail. Suffice to say that when British Governments believe that inflation or economic activity can be influenced by changes in the price of money, *i.e.* the rate of interest, they naturally turn to the money market as the place to take action. And they use the Bank of England as their main instrument.

Since 1998, as we explained in Chapter 2, the Bank of England has been given full responsibility for the level of interest rates. The Government, through the Treasury, provides inflation targets and the Bank of England is given operational independence to ensure that the target is met. (If inflation deviates more than 1% on either side of the target—at present 2.5%—the Governor is obliged to write an open letter to the Chancellor explaining the deviation.) The Bank's decision-making on the level of interest rates is undertaken through regular monthly meetings of the Monetary Policy Committee, chaired by the Governor. Its decision to change or not to change the Bank's base rate is published immediately. The Committee's deliberations are minuted and published within six weeks.

The change in the interest rate announced by the Bank of England is in effect the rate which immediately affects its own dealings with the money market and, thereby, influences the whole pattern of interest rates set by commercial banks, building societies and other financial institutions—eventually affecting you and me. These decisions are also backed up by the Bank's daily operations in the money market, which we must now begin to explain in more detail.

The Bank of England operates by directly influencing the cost of money to the banking system. It does this by keeping the banking system short of money and then lending the banks the money they need at an interest rate which the Bank decides. The basic point is that, since the Bank is banker to the banking system, transactions between commercial banks (ultimately reflecting total transactions between the

The Financial System

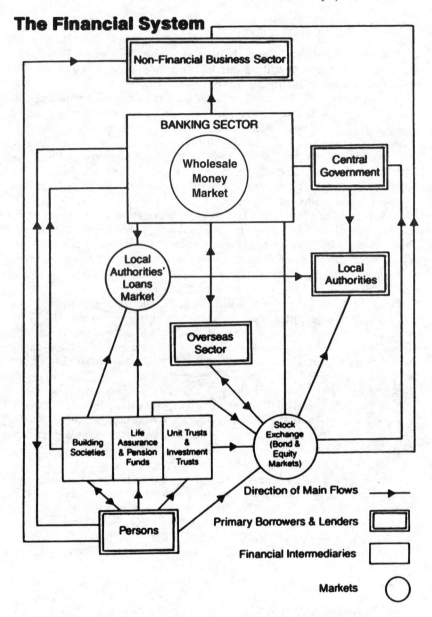

This diagram, prepared by Barclays Bank has been adapted to summarise (i) how one sector of the City relates to another, and (ii) how money flows to and from City markets to the general public and other parts of the economy.

private sector and the Government) are finally settled between accounts held at the Bank of England by the main settlement banks, *i.e.* the 22 banks which are members of the wholesale clearing system.

Normally, the operation of the Government's accounts results in the settlement banks starting each day with a shortage of funds. It is the way in which the Bank of England relieves this shortage (or not) that influences interest rates, and we are now in a position to see exactly how this works in practice.

The Bank's daily operations, known as "open market operations", to relieve the shortage are conducted in the money market through dealings with eligible banks, building societies, securities firms and the remaining discount houses. They are invited to apply for funds by the sale of Treasury bills, other eligible bills and, more recently, gilt repo.

This daily ritual begins as follows. The Bank publishes each morning at about 9.45 a.m., and if necessary revises at noon and 2.30 p.m., its estimates of the shortage or surplus of funds in the market that day. The estimate incorporates all the information available to the Bank about the prospective flows of money through the system, of which those between the Government and the banks are of particular importance. If a shortage is eventually indicated the Bank will be prepared to supply the funds by "open market operations" with the financial institutions *at a rate of interest of its own choosing*. If a surplus is indicated the Bank will operate to "mop up" the surplus.

Out of these transactions emerges a pattern of short term interest rates in bills as well as a reasonably clear signal about official hopes and intentions. The banks react accordingly, as do the building societies, and make their own decisions about their lending and borrowing rates. In this way the Bank's operations gradually seep through the financial system and ultimately through the whole economy.

8. Foreign Exchange

Need for Foreign Currency

You take a holiday in France. I buy shares in a Japanese company. A friend sells equipment to an importer in Pittsburg. The Government lends money to Bangladesh. In each case and at some time, these different actions will lead to a need to exchange pounds into a foreign currency or the other way round. So we must now explore how the City helps these transactions to take place.

Several practical questions arise at the outset. Where do the French francs come from? How does the supplier of Japanese shares get paid? Where does the American importer get hold of the pounds to pay for the equipment? Who helps the Government to transfer monetary aid to Bangladesh?

These are the first questions, and we shall do our best to answer them as we go along. But they lead immediately to several more fundamental ones. Which parts of the City are involved in obtaining the foreign currency? Where do they do it? Who decides how many French francs, American dollars or Japanese yen we get for our pounds?

The short answer is the foreign exchange market. In the time-span of only one generation, the London market has been transformed from a leisurely top-hatted twice-weekly meeting at the Royal Exchange to the present electronic market, spanning the globe on a 24-hour basis. Yet one thing at least has remained unchanged: the principle on which it works. Foreign currencies are now switched from one to another at a price which fluctuates second by second; and the place where all this takes place is no different from a market in apples or oranges. When pounds are in demand the price goes up: when pounds are sold the price goes down. The only complication worth watching (and one which distinguishes it from other markets) is that the price can be expressed in either currency. The exchange rate, or price, can be shown as so many francs, dollars etc. to one pound, or so many pounds, dollars, etc., to 100 francs.

Why Exchange is Needed

Before explaining the way the market works in any detail, however, we need to consider what leads to these demands for different currencies, and how one kind of demand differs from another.

Tourists   Each year more foreigners visit Greece, Italy and Spain than Greeks, Italians and Spaniards visit other countries. From June to September their beaches and cities are thronged with foreigners. Where do they obtain the drachmae, lire and pesetas they need? The answer, basically, is that tourists ask their banks and the banks, in turn, obtain some foreign exchange from other tourists and get the rest through the foreign exchange market. Incidentally, we use the phrase "foreign currency" here to mean either foreign bank notes and cash or foreign bank deposits. The foreign exchange market, basically, concerns itself with bank deposits, between banks, but specialist banks (such as Brown Shipley in London and Swiss Bank Corporation in Zurich) act as wholesale suppliers of notes to other banks.

Importers and Exporters   An importer of Japanese cars in California will need to have enough yen at his disposal to pay for the imports, or the Japanese car exporters, if he receives dollars for the cars he has sold, will need to exchange the dollars into yen. Either way there is an extra demand for yen at some point and an additional sale of dollars. As we shall see in a moment, there may be a delay in these transactions because of the use of the forward market. Similar sales and purchases will be going on all round the world. Some of the currency needed may be found within the same bank. In other cases, the bank will have to find what it needs in the market-place, that is, in the foreign exchange market.

Investors   The demand for currency need not be confined to the sale of services or manufactured goods. Foreign currency will also be needed to purchase a foreign subsidiary or simply a few shares in a foreign company on the New York or Tokyo stock exchange. In recent years the demand for American dollars has been boosted considerably by such purchases. Once again the demands for individual currencies will occasionally be met within an individual bank or security house, but the additional need will have to be satisfied in the foreign exchange market.

Payments by Government The involvement of Governments in making foreign payments has grown dramatically in the past quarter century. At one time only the upkeep of embassies and troop movements led to any significant volume of official payments overseas. Now governmental involvement covers embassy costs, aid of all kinds, defence costs (including the sale and purchase of armaments on a huge scale) as well as the sale of gold and other national assets. These transactions too lead to demands on the foreign exchange market. To sum up, we have, so far, identified several features of the demands on the foreign exchange market:

   (i) Thousands of billions of international payments arise annually because of the need to buy foreign services and foreign goods; to invest abroad; and to make official payments overseas.

  (ii) Some of the need for foreign currency, arising from this bewildering array of payments, will be immediately offset by similar payments the other way.

 (iii) The banks will meet the demand for individual currencies through their operations in the foreign exchange market, always subject to their own prudence and, in London, the rules of the Bank of England.

 (iv) The banks operating in the foreign exchange market are primarily concerned with switching bank deposits in one currency into bank deposits in another currency. They will, however, provide notes and cash, from specialised wholesale banks, where these are needed.

The Market

We finally come to the heart of the matter: the market itself. Unlike several City markets in the past it has no central meeting place but is scattered all round the Square Mile, the participants linked to each other electronically by telephone, telex, information screens and electronic matching systems.

Who are the participants? At present some 350 banks are permitted to join the market, though the main activity takes place in around 50 of the banks, along with twelve or thirteen broking firms (of which seven are specialists in certain currencies).

The individual offices are remarkably equipped. Banks of screens surround each dealer, some containing general economic information, some recording changes in exchange rates and interest rates. Telexes and teleprinters are both prominent. So, increasingly, are the new computerised systems capable of matching foreign exchange deals.

HSBC Midland dealing room (Brian Capon/British Bankers' Association)

But still at the centre of it all are the ubiquitous telephone equipment and computer screens, specially designed for the purpose, with winking lights and the other marvels of the modern age, linking one bank with another, with the broking firms and the Bank of England in London and with other dealers in other centres overseas. Electronic broking systems have also been introduced, now accounting for about a quarter of spot dealings.

Each set of dealers in the large banks concentrates on individual currencies, such as the dollar, the mark or the yen. Each bank will have its own buying and selling needs as it begins each day. Some will be on behalf of customers; some on behalf of itself, since it will need to adjust the stock of currencies it maintains for its own purposes. Each dealer will also be responding to calls from others.

As the dealing day begins in London, calls to and from Tokyo, Hong Kong and Singapore will mingle with London and European business. The Middle East centres too will be joining in. Shortly after lunchtime, New York calls will begin to be put through and, later in the afternoon, early business from Los Angeles and San Francisco.

One deal will lead to another. The latest news (of economic trends in the U.S. and Japan; or rises in interest rates in Paris) will bring a further flurry of business. Forward transactions will affect current exchange rates. The incomprehensible jargon; shouts across the room; the winking lights; the need to log each transaction often running into millions—all suggest the need for alertness, stamina and youth. And in fact most dealers these days are in their twenties and thirties.

How the Market Works

We need to distinguish between the brokers and the banks (*i.e.* the dealers) at the outset. The brokers earn a fee from bringing buyers and sellers together and they do this by providing regular information on the different rates (buying and selling) offered by different banks. Banks can, of course, deal direct with each other.

The rates quoted these days are invariably against one currency, the U.S. dollar. They are called spot rates of exchange and imply that the two currencies concerned will be exchanged on the second working day after the transactions. Two prices are offered by a bank, or a broker on behalf of a bank. For example, a bank will say it will deal in sterling at $1.5995–1.6005. This means it is prepared to buy pounds at a rate of $1.5995 to the pound and to sell pounds at $1.6005 to the pound.

A bank wanting to sell dollars on behalf of a commercial client will receive a range of different possibilities through a broker (or occasionally by direct contact) and will quickly decide which is best. But the amounts on offer may not tally and this imbalance may lead to other deals. And so the market's business will continue.

Forward Market

This, however, is only part of the full story. Exporters and importers will often need to bear in mind that they will be receiving, or paying, foreign currency three, or even six months later, because of delays in deliveries of goods. They will not know, though they may have a view about, the likely exchange rate in three or six months time.

The question facing a British exporter who has agreed a dollar price for his exports at the present rate of exchange between pounds and dollars, is whether he will receive the same amount in pounds when the American importer makes his payment three months hence. If the pound is weaker, he will receive more pounds for the agreed amount of dollars. If it is stronger, he will receive less. How can he avoid this kind of future risk? The answer lies in the use of forward exchange.

He can sell American dollars forward at a price. It is in essence the cost of an insurance policy, thus protecting him against any change in the exchange rate.

This is the problem facing the exporter. Now let's see how his decision to sell his dollars forward affects the dealers in the exchange market. In order to meet the exporter's needs to sell his dollars, say, three months forward, the bank dealing in the foreign exchange market can accommodate him in two different ways:

(i) It can borrow dollars for three months, sell them immediately for sterling and put the pounds on deposit for three months. After three months the sterling deposit will be available to pay the exporter, and the bank can repay its dollar loan with the dollars which it arranged to buy from the exporter.

(ii) Alternatively, the bank can buy *spot* sterling and then arrange what is known as a "swap", exchanging the *spot* sterling for three months' forward sterling. In this case, the two spot sterling deals cancel each other out and the bank is left with a contract to receive sterling in three months time. These match the contract with the exporter.

This is all rather complex, even to explain. But it is worth stressing two simple points: that the aim is to provide the exporter with a method of covering his exposure to foreign exchange fluctuations and that the introduction of a "swap" arrangement by the bank (the second of the two lines of action open to the bank set out above) is based on the use of the short-term money market, which we explained in Chapter 7. It becomes clear, therefore, that it is easier to arrange forward currency deals in currencies where an extensive range of short-term securities and instruments exists. These are basically dollars, pounds and Deutschmarks.

Size of the Market

London's foreign exchange market now has the world's largest turnover, with New York running at about 55 per cent of London's total. The reason for this is partly historical (the widespread use of sterling in the past and the expertise acquired over the years), partly geographical (as we have noted, London is placed neatly in the time zones between the Far East and North America) and partly structural (London has far more foreign banks than other centres). Turnover is colossal. The Bank of England puts it at over $600 billion *a day* in London alone. About 65 per cent of this total is accounted for by forward business. Since world trade in goods and services amounts to only a fraction of this each working day, turnover in the exchange market between market participants is clearly boosted for other reasons.

The reasons are not far to seek. In the first place, the lending banks making up the market generate exchange business of their own in their capacity as market-makers in different currencies, assuming that they have sufficient stocks for their purpose. On top of this, the world's central banks also operate in the market (often through chosen commercial banks) not only in their role as custodians of national exchange reserves but in attempting to smooth out excessive fluctuations in the market. Finally, as the U.S. dollar is the pivotal currency, transactions between other currencies may involve an intermediate exchange into dollars, again enlarging total turnover. Whatever the reason for this extra turnover, it helps to provide the essential liquidity needed in any active market.

9. The Euro and the City

The launch of the Euro on January 4, 1999 was the culmination of years of discussion (and dispute) within the European Union. In the event 11 European currencies merged together to establish one currency on that date. They were the currencies of Germany, France, Italy, Spain, Netherlands, Belgium, Austria, Portugal, Finland, Ireland, and Luxembourg. Conversion rates between these individual currencies and the Euro were irrevocably fixed. Foreign exchange operations in the new currency began in the exchange markets. Thus the three-stage timetable hammered out under the Maastricht Treaty, under which Britain and Denmark were given opt-outs, was firmly adhered to. In addition Sweden decided not to join and Greece was deemed ineligible.

The next steps were just as firmly set out . Newly designed Euro bank notes and coins were to be issued on January 1, 2002 and the legal status of national bank notes and coins to be cancelled on July 1, 2002. Thus in the period between 1999 and 2002 the Euro would be introduced by banks in the 11 countries concerned, though not in notes and coins. Prices in national currencies and Euros would be shown side by side, and large companies would begin to issue invoices in Euros.

Any currency needs a single Government to back it up. Thus behind the Euro launch and the start of a new single currency lay inevitable political decisions and institutions within the European Union. The clear implication was a further move towards a federal Europe (one of several reasons given for Britain's decision to defer entry). Thus a new independent European Central Bank was established in Frankfurt with responsibility for interest rates and a single monetary policy. In addition a new Pact for Stability and Growth was agreed between E.U. Member States. This provided for sanctions against any country participating in the Euro in cases of failure to respect the budgetary criteria (see below) they had adopted for inclusion in the Euro. All this meant that the Euro countries had individually given up direct control in setting their own monetary policy and interest rate and were constrained in pursuing their own fiscal policies.

The budgetary criteria adopted by every country accepted as a member of the single currency are:

- The public budget deficit should not exceed 3 per cent of GDP unless it has already undergone a substantial reduction and any excess can be considered exceptional.
- Public debt should not exceed 60 per cent of GDP unless it is falling at a satisfactory rate towards this ratio.
- Inflation should not be more than 1.5 percentage points above the three Member States with the best price stability performances.
- Long term interest rates should not be more than 2 percentage points above rates in the three Member States with the best performance on price stability.

The Pound and the Euro

The question whether Britain should join the single currency is still being debated. The Chancellor of the Exchequer set out the Government's position in 1997 when he said that five economic tests should be applied and satisfied before the pound merged with the Euro. These were:

  (i) Whether the U.K. economy has achieved sustainable convergence with the economies of the single currency;
 (ii) Whether there is sufficient flexibility in the U.K. economy to adapt to change and other unexpected events;
(iii) Whether joining the single currency would create better conditions for businesses to make long-term decisions to invest in the U.K.
 (iv) The impact membership would have on the U.K. financial services industry;
  (v) Ultimately whether joining the single currency would be good for employment.

Subsequently the Government has issued what it calls a National Changeover Plan under which it sets out what preparations should be made between now and the next Parliament if the country is to join the single currency in the next Parliament, once the five tests have been met. The timetable for such preparations for U.K. entry go as follows: (i) the Government makes a decision to join; (ii) the Government seeks approval by a national referendum; (iii) the pound joins the single currency; (iv) Euro notes and coins are introduced; (v) sterling is finally withdrawn. The Government has said that the whole of this process, from decision to join to the final withdrawal of sterling, would take three years, four months.

It will be seen that the five tests put forward by the Chancellor are economic ones. They can probably be summed up by assessing whether Britain's economic history and geography, as a free trading island economy, will fit easily (as part of a fixed exchange rate regime) alongside continental economies, without undue stresses and strains. All this needs to be considered. But the debate on whether to join or not has, basically, revolved around the political question of whether Britain should join a federal united Europe or a looser coupling of nation states: in effect the question of how much sovereignty the country is willing to lose in order to co-operate with Europe.

That sovereignty will be lost in economic and monetary areas does not mean that economic issues are the sole test. The two sovereignty questions to be considered are whether the country (and particularly industry) wishes to leave any future decision on monetary policy and interest rate to a non-elected European Central Bank in Frankfurt and whether the country wishes to pass the fiscal restraints of the Stability Pact to an equally non-elected European Commission in Brussels. What might suit Germany or Spain may not suit Britain or France, etc., etc. This is the main political issue to be faced.

Impact on the City

We must now face the issue of the Euro's impact on the City. The question for the City of London has been how the single currency has affected, and will affect, its major markets. Some people have argued that the City would lose out to other European centres, such as Frankfurt, especially since the European Central Bank is established there. It has been used as a reason for an early British entry into the single currency.

What has happened so far? The major feature before the Euro launch was the City's determination to prepare every market for the changeover to the Euro, without the pound as a member. Detailed preparations were deliberately co-ordinated by the Bank of England and by the time of the launch the City's markets had ensured that its wholesale trading, payments systems and settlement facilities were able to handle the new Euro—just like any other currency.

As a result, City institutions and traders were ready to offer Euro-denominated financial services at the start of trading on January 1, 1999. They were able to quote prices in the full range of Euro-denominated financial instruments. They stood ready to make whole-sale Euro payments for British or foreign clients; and they were able to settle the full range of Euro securities. Considering that the City has been dealing in foreign transactions for centuries and has deliberately built its current structure on Euro-currencies of all denominations since the 1960's (see Chapter 10), such flexibility was a natural, even logical, step.

If Britain does eventually join the single currency, several areas for further treatment have been identified. They are: (i) the Government would have to consider converting gilt-edged issues into Euro-based paper on or shortly after joining; (ii) those issuing and trading in sterling securities would have to consider changing their face value into Euros, as well as consider other technical points such as security prices and methods of calculating interest; (iii) the Bank of England would have to consider its monetary policy instruments to bring them into line with those introduced by the European Central Bank; and (iv) the inter-bank payment system known as "CHAPS" would have to be integrated. (It is calculated that the Euro inter-bank payments system would have to cope with an increase in transactions from 15,000–25,000 payments per day to around 170,000.) All these changes, apart from the CHAPS changes, might be accomplished in or around twelve months. The CHAPS adjustment might take two years.

European Competition

In the year prior to the launch of the Euro, reports of the preparations being made in Frankfurt and Paris gave the impression that Frankfurt (and to a lesser extent Paris) would soon be rivalling London as Europe's prime financial centre. Moves to consolidate the financial futures market in Frankfurt (merging with one in Zurich and extending development outside Europe), to extend the investment banking arms of Germany's major banks and to develop the Frankfurt Bourse all focussed attention on prospects outside London. The positioning of the European Central Bank in Frankfurt added to the feeling that London would quickly lose her position if the pound remained outside the single currency.

The assessment of Europe's rivals for the financial crown will go on. But in making such assessments, the present position of the contenders should not be ignored. Whatever criteria are used, it becomes clear that London and New York as prime financial centres are at present without rival in the world. New York has the biggest domestic turnover of almost any centre and some of the largest financial players in the world, while London leads the field in specialised international services over a remarkable spectrum.

To turn from these two to other centres in Europe is instructive. Take the current international statistics for London, Frankfurt and Paris alone:

- London, with 556 *foreign banks*, has <u>double</u> the number of those in Frankfurt (231) and more than Frankfurt and Paris (173) put together.
- *Foreign exchange* turnover in London, at $637 billion, is <u>over six times</u> that in Frankfurt ($94 billion) and nearly <u>ten times</u> that in Paris.
- The *turnover in foreign equities* in London accounts for 58 per cent of the world total, compared with <u>no more than 3 per cent</u> in Frankfurt, Paris and Tokyo combined.
- London has 526 *foreign equity listings*, <u>nearly double</u> the number in Frankfurt (229) and well over double the Paris total (193).
- London's share of *international banking transactions* (19 per cent), the world's largest, is <u>more than Frankfurt and Paris together</u>.
- London is now the world's leading *gold bullion* centre, with a daily turnover of between $10 billion and $13 billion. Neither Frankfurt nor Paris can claim to be significant gold centres.
- London's *insurance market* (Lloyd's and the companies) has the <u>largest share</u> of the international marine market (Tokyo is second place) and of the international aviation market (New York second). Paris and Frankfurt do not underwrite such amounts of international business.
- London claims to undertake a <u>half</u> of the world's *shipping freight fixtures* and, in Lloyd's Register of Shipping, has the world's premium ship classification society. Frankfurt and Paris are not maritime centres.
- In *derivative transactions* London has the <u>largest turnover</u> in "over the counter" deals and LIFFE is running <u>neck and neck</u> with Frankfurt, though both lag behind Chicago and New York.

These factual points simply illustrate the lead that London at present enjoys and seem to indicate that, whether the pound joins the single currency or not, other European centres are bound to find it difficult to replace London's vast range of international services. What other characteristics London possesses will be explored in Chapter 15.

10. Euro-currencies

What the Market is

Forty-five years ago the Euro-currency market did not exist. Now it is a fund of international borrowing worth over $950 billion. It probably began in Paris, was nurtured and developed in London and now links the leading financial centres of the world.

It is based on a simple and familiar principle: the use of someone else's debts to finance developments world-wide. As we found in Chapter 2, the IOUs of the Irish, once they were regarded as acceptable, in the midst of a bank strike, began to be used as a means of payment by others. So in the international arena, dollars or other currencies, accumulating in the hands of foreigners, began to be lent to others again because they were acceptable. In other words, currency deposits accumulating outside their country of origin, which are basically that country's debts, are being used as the basis of future loans.

The source of such funds will become clearer if we take the case of a French exporter earning dollars from the shipment of goods to the United States. Let's assume that he sells tractors to an American farmer and earns $500,000. He can do several things with the dollars:

- buy American goods or services;
- invest them in American stocks or shares on Wall Street;
- ask his bank to exchange them for French francs;
- exchange them for other foreign currencies, yen, pounds, marks, etc.;
- buy other foreign goods or services;
- hold them in an account outside the USA for future use.

If he chooses one of the first two options, $500,000 will end up back in the United States and thus be extinguished as a foreign-held debt of the U.S. But if he chooses any of the next three options, the dollars will probably be transferred to another foreign holder or bank who will then face the same original options.

The rapidity with which a major international financial market can be established is graphically shown by the first use in print of the word "Euro-dollar".

As this chapter explains, the market in Euro-dollars had developed in the late 1950s. Towards the middle of October 1960, as Financial Editor of *The Times*, I was preparing an annual survey for *The Times*, summing up both the previous year and the prospects, in one of the world major financial centres. "Challenge of the City's New Freedom: Problems of the Sixties" was the heading.

Turning to the City of London's financial innovations, I began to describe a "completely new" market which, I explained, "illustrates the true versatility of the City as much as anything that has happened in recent years". The article went on: "This is the *so-called Euro-dollar market* . . . basically this is a market where dollar deposits earned and owned by foreigners (mostly European as the name implies) can be left and still earn a higher rate of interest than is available in New York".

I was in effect describing the birth of a market which now dominates the world's financial centres. What I did not realise was that this was the first time the phrase "Euro-dollar market" had been used in public print. It took another twelve years before this "world first" was finally recognised by the 1972 Supplement to the *Oxford English Dictionary*.

It is when the last option is chosen, *i.e.* the placing of the dollars in a foreign currency account for future use, either by the original earner of the dollars or by a subsequent recipient of them, that they become available for use by banks in the so-called Euro-currency market. At this point the $500,000 can be lent to others for three, six or twelve months. They have, in current terminology, become active Euro-dollars. If the original exporter had earned yen or marks, and had deposited them, in the same way, outside their country of origin, we would call them Euro-yen or Euro-marks.

How it Began

We now need to explore how, why and when Euro-dollars, Euro-yen, Euro-marks emerged in the first place and why the "Euro-" tag has always been attached to them.

We have to go back to the Europe of the mid-1950s to find the answer. Marshal Aid dollars were flowing to Europe. Its major economies were beginning to emerge successfully from the destruction of war. The stirrings of the future Common Market were already discernible. Trading and currency barriers were being slowly dismantled.

As a result, Europe's foreign earnings were rising again and the dollar deficit it had been plagued with for close on a decade was moving into surplus. U.S. dollars were thus accumulating in European hands, at a time when the freedom to switch currencies across national frontier was returning.

Our earlier example of the choice facing the French exporter, earning surplus dollars, was becoming commonplace. Enterprising financial institutions began to recognise new credit opportunities, and to find ways of using the spare dollars. Where the first on lending of such surplus dollar deposits began is still disputed, but it is now generally accepted that the Soviet-owned bank in Paris, Banque Commerciale pour l'Europe du Nord, is a leading contender for the title. Its telex "answer-back" code was "Euro-bank" and, when it was offering dollars, the term "Euro-dollar" was an easy adaptation.

Yet the Euro-dollar market we know was not developed in Paris. The vast international credit potential lying behind the dollars accumulating in European hands was first recognised in London, not Paris, primarily among the British overseas and merchant banks and the branches of American banks. They quickly began to bid (that is, offer higher interest rates) for the surplus dollars and were helped by an official quirk in New York. Under the financial regulation ("Q"), introduced to curb excessive interest rates for house loans, banks in New York were prevented from offering interest rates above a certain level.

So what New York prevented, London encouraged, and by the end of the 1950s a new source of international finance had been tapped and was being slowly developed in London. But it was not immediately recognised and it was not until 1960 that the first public reference to the phrase "Euro-dollar" was made. The first recorded reference, according to the 1972 Supplement to the *Oxford English Dictionary*, was in *The Times'* financial review of October 24, 1960. [see pages 79–80]

How it Works

A new source of international money had been discovered, just when the world economic boom of the sixties and early seventies was beginning. Soon foreign banks were flocking to London to take advantage of these new facilities. The nucleus of the Euro-currency market was quickly formed and the present-day techniques emerged from the simple three-month and six-month dollar credits of those early days.

In the early 1960s, the Euro-currency market divided itself into two different sectors: (i) that providing *Euro-currency loans*; and (ii) that providing *Eurobonds*. The first was in essence a credit market supplied directly by banks; the second was an international capital market offered by banks as an alternative to the national capital markets.

The distinction between international credit supplied by banks and an international capital market based on the issue of market instruments (Eurobonds, etc.) is worth nothing, for, as we shall see in a moment, the dividing line between the two has since got more and more blurred.

(i) Euro-currency Loans In the case of loans, the necessary currency funds were originally sought from holders on a three-month or six-month basis. Through the use of what are called "roll-over" techniques (which amount to little more than the renewal of existing deposits), funds were held for longer periods, thus enabling the banks acting as intermediaries to lengthen the Euro-currency loans to borrowers. In the early years such loans were extended up to two years; but, with the introduction of new techniques (especially the use of variable interest rates), the length of loans moved to five years, then seven years and beyond.

The interest rate offered to holders of external currency deposits is based on what is known as LIBOR, that is the London Interbank Offered Rate. This rate naturally varies. When these funds are lent to borrowers in the Euro-currency market, a margin is added to the LIBOR rate to cover administrative costs and the potential risks.

Borrowers pay a flexible rate of interest and can take up as much, or as little, of the loan as they wish.

(ii) Eurobonds Just as the American Regulation Q gave an unexpected boost to the development of the Euro-dollar market outside the United States, so the imposition of an interest equalisation tax on foreign bond issues in New York in 1963 (which raised the cost of borrowing money there to foreign borrowers) was a powerful boost to Eurobonds.

Instead of issuing dollar bonds in New York, international banks, spurred on by their successes with the Euro-currency loans, turned to issuing dollar bonds in several centres simultaneously. The first of such issues was arranged by S.G. Warburg, the London merchant bank. It was a 6 year $15 million bond issue for Autostrade Italiane at 5.5 per cent. Others followed. They were the first Eurobonds. American banks in particular were encouraged to issue such bonds abroad which, for close on a decade, they were unable to do at home.

Eurobonds were originally mainly in dollars. Thus foreign corporations were able to raise fixed-interest-rate dollar loans, in the form of bonds, in, say, London and Luxembourg simultaneously. They would be for a fixed period, from five to fifteen years. And the international banks naturally tapped some of the same Euro-currency market sources for their potential purchasers: foreign corporations and governments but, above all, rich individuals attracted by the freedom from withholding tax and the anonymity of bearer bonds.

Where the Market Operates

Thus, within a decade culminating in the mid-1960s, two new additions were added to the world's financial instruments: Euro-currency loans and Eurobonds. Both have taken their place alongside the nationally based credits and bonds.

In each case, international banks operating out of leading financial centres such as London, New York, Frankfurt, Zurich, Paris and Tokyo and out of more recently established centres such as Hong Kong, Singapore, Nassau, Bahrain and Luxembourg, have co-operated together in syndicates.

Euro-credits have usually involved one international bank as lead manager, with one or two others as co-managers and often a score or more other banks as participants. Similarly with Eurobonds, one bank will be lead manager and scores of others will act as underwriters of the issue.

But where, you may ask, is the Euro-currency market itself? Where exactly does it operate? There is in fact no market-place. It is held together by telephone, telex, fax and e-mail, and operates, simultaneously, from several centres.

In London, where it was developed and where its major developments are still initiated, day-to-day activities, particularly the deposit-raising, take place in the foreign exchange operations rooms of the major banks. But the construction of Euro-syndicated loans and Eurobonds goes on in a variety of bank parlours, and security houses, linked together by world-wide telex, fax and E-mail.

The *secondary* market in Eurobonds, and later variants such as Floating Rate Notes (that is, where existing bonds, notes or other instruments are traded) takes place between banks and security houses, largely in London, New York and Luxembourg. All Eurobond issues are quoted on a European Stock Exchange.

The Borrowers

So far we have been primarily concerned with the world banks supplying and building up these new international markets. They were naturally crucial in the initial development of the markets. Later, however, the needs of the borrowers began to play a more significant influence in market developments.

The original borrowers were the credit-worthy multinationals, large industrial companies and governments of the industrialised west. Individual central banks too used the Euro-currency market as a safety valve, sometimes lending surplus dollars, sometimes borrowing. All this was in the economic boom period of the sixties and early seventies.

Following the dramatic rise in oil prices in 1973–74, however, new financial problems arose. Huge currency surpluses began to accumulate in the Middle East, and western banks were urged to "re-cycle" (*i.e.* to borrow and re-lend) them to the needy countries of the developing world, through the technique of syndicated loans. Otherwise, it was said, economic and social disaster would spread throughout South America and South East Asia.

International banks initially dithered, wondering (rightly as it turned out) whether it would be wise to borrow such surpluses and re-lend them to the developing world and thus take on the political risk, rather than persuade the Middle East holders to lend direct. But the combination of competition (if Bank A would not do it, Bank B certainly would) and the persuasive powers of politicians and commentators alike, calmed all doubts and in a space of six years, Euro-credits of all kinds flowed to the developing world and the Soviet bloc. At a later stage, the need to spread the risk on loan portfolios was a further stimulus to lending.

We now know the results. International banks clearly lent too much to the wrong countries at the wrong time. By the autumn of 1982, some of the largest borrowers—Poland, Mexico, Brazil, Argentina—were having difficulties in making the regular interest payments, let alone repaying loans when due.

The debts built up so rapidly in the late 1970s and early 1980s through Euro-curency lending thus left their mark on lenders and borrowers alike. Although the capital basis of leading international banks was undermined as provisions had to be put aside to meet potential losses, Japan's payment surpluses in some ways replaced the oil country surpluses, and continuing U.S. deficits left surplus dollars available for international lending. At the same time past borrowers were keen to lengthen repayment periods and to re-arrange their future liabilities. Industrial borrowers tended to replace Sovereign country borrowers.

New Techniques

Thus the climate was ripe for the introduction of new lending techniques and more flexible financial instruments. The Euro-markets responded in the 1980s and early 1990s with a bewildering array of new processes, with equally bewildering names from "swaps" to FRNs and ECPs and from RUFs, PUFs and NIFs to SNIFs, MOFs and PIFs. The big banks now spend much time in trying to tailor new techniques to the needs of their international customers.

Text books and individual conferences are now devoted to many of these techniques. All we will try to explain briefly, therefore, is what some of the main techniques attempt to do for the lender or the borrower.

(i) Swaps   There are interest rate swaps and currency swaps. Both help a borrower to change the character of his existing debts, particularly for the purposes of hedging risks. This can be achieved either by avoiding an unnecessary concentration of, say, dollar debts or by changing the proportions of debts with fixed or floating interest rates.

A *currency swap* is usually arranged through a bank, acting as intermediary. One borrower may have excessive dollar debts; another may have excessive Swiss franc debts. The bank can help each borrower to switch a proportion of its debts into the other currency, partly through the use of matching formal exchange contracts, and partly through each borrower's ability to forward the appropriate currency for each other. Each borrower is in effect borrowing the currency in which its credit is best and offering the terms to the other.

An *interest rate swap* can be done directly between a borrower and a bank. A bank finds it is easier, and cheaper, to borrow fixed-rate credit. An industrial corporation, however, will get better terms from floating-rate credit. So in such a swap, each borrows for the other. In other words, each party is borrowing in the market (floating rate or fixed rate) in which its credit is best and offering the terms to the other (*i.e.* swapping credit positions).

To understand how each swap is actually carried out needs patience, numerous diagrams and an expert (and friendly) banker. And do not feel too intimidated when you hear of such things as "swaptions", which are a mixture of a swap and an option, "caps", "floors" and "collars". Just readily assume that they are other examples of this growing market's ingenuity and flexibility.

Although we have introduced the technique of "swaps" here, its use has formed part of the dramatic expansion in so-called "derivatives" which we shall be explaining in more detail in Chapter 13. Turnover in swaps of all kinds now runs into trillions of dollars.

(ii) Floating Rate Notes (FRNs)   As we noted earlier, Euro-credits based on short-term deposits were transformed into larger credits by the simple process of rolling them over, *i.e.* renewing them at regular intervals at flexible rates of interest. The floating rate note is the result of introducing similar interest rate flexibilities into the bond market. A company borrowing money on such an issue is thus not tied to a fixed rate of interest; nor indeed is the lender.

Although FRNs were first introduced in 1970, only in the last few years have they been used in large volume. Banks themselves have recently been among the main borrowers.

The maturity of FRNs extend from five to fifteen years, and even longer. Interest rates are based on an agreed margin (dependent on the borrower's credit rating) over LIBOR (see earlier), and are adjusted at regular intervals.

(iii) RUFs, NIFs, MOFs, etc.   These various facilities have different descriptions, *e.g.* revolving underwriting facilities (RUFs), note issuing facilities (NIFs), Multi-Option Facilities (MOFs), etc., etc., but their aim, and the principles behind them, are much the same. Borrowers are receiving a basic, medium-term flexible facility. This in turn is financed by the purchase by investors of short-term notes, usually of three or six months' duration. The banks ensure that the short-term notes link together to provide a medium-term facility. They do this by underwriting the underlying short-term notes (*i.e.* by promising to buy any unpurchased notes) and by providing a stand-by credit. The term "Note issuance facility", or NIF, is often used to cover all the different variants, such as Euro-note facilities, or revolving underwriting facilities (RUFs).

(iv) Euro-commercial Paper   Commercial paper, basically short-term (*i.e.* less than nine months) promissory instruments which do not have a bankers' endorsement and are not necessarily linked to trading transactions, has been firmly established as a way of financing American industry for decades. Its use on a wider international scale, what we now call Euro-commercial paper, only began in the 1980s. It was in essence an extension of the Euro-note market which itself, as we have seen, grew out of the Euro-syndicated loan market.

(v) Euro-Equities   Although the Euro-currency and Eurobond markets were originally built on the provision of credit and fixed interest capital, it was clearly only a matter of time before domestic equities (that is, the issue of ordinary shares) would be followed by international issues, now called Euro-equities. They have expanded rapidly in recent years and now offer large international corporations an additional source of equity finance.

Widening of the Market

We noted earlier how the Euro-currency market had originally split into two sections in the early 1960s, one supplying credits (Euro-syndicated loans) through banks direct to borrowers, the other providing capital market instruments (Eurobonds). For a number of reasons, as we have already indicated, this distinction became slowly—on occasions dramatically—more and more blurred; as did the distinction between Eurobonds and foreign bonds in domestic markets.

One of the major turning points was the third world debt problem, brought to a head by the Mexican crisis of 1982. Other factors played their part too. The world's banks, who bore the brunt of the debt crisis, naturally turned away from direct bank lending and encouraged what is now known as the "securitisation" of past and future debts, *i.e.* a growing reliance on financial instruments which could be sold, and thus spread the underlying risks through the market-place, rather than on direct loans from the banks themselves. In other words the basis of a medium term Euro-credit could be a note, which is marketable and transferable, rather than a bank loan. Thus banks were more able to adjust their lending to suit their existing liabilities. The variety of new instruments we have tried to outline was one of the results. The total of Eurobond issues rose from $20 billion in 1980 to over $600 billion in 1998. In the latter year Euro-syndicated loans amounted to only $350 million.

The Eurobond market, which was originally quite distinct from foreign loans in domestic markets, is now increasingly embracing such issues. Tax and other obstacles in the domestic markets, which two decades ago were still limiting foreign issues, have slowly disappeared. (Harmonisation of taxes within the European Union, if pursued with vigour, could still undermine London's position, by adjusting withholding taxes.) Exchange controls have been relaxed in various countries. As a result the term Eurobond has now been extended to include what are basically foreign bonds issued in domestic markets, provided that they are distributed to international investors by international syndicates.

London's role in these various market developments has remained dominant. The Euro-currency markets had initially developed in the Square Mile. The largest share of Euro-syndicated credits was arranged in London. It is now estimated that two thirds of secondary transaction in Eurobonds take place in London. In recent years London has also gained 60 per cent of the primary issuing business in Eurobonds. And the accompanying swap market (80 per cent of Eurobond business is now accompanied by currency swaps) is basically divided between London and New York.

11. The Gold Market

Markets in gold bring together rich governments and thrifty peasants; dentists and investors; capitalist banks and Socialist trading organisations. They are markets in a commodity and markets in money. Most leading financial centres have one.

What Gold is

Gold is a unique commodity. It remains the basic store of value in the world—for governments and individuals. It is widely regarded as the main bulwark against rampant inflation, depreciating currencies, revolution and invasion. It has a glamour possessed by no other metal. Yet its price, whether in terms of other commodities or paper money, can be as volatile as anything else.

It is a metal with remarkable qualities: soft enough to be turned into beautiful jewellery; hard enough to be used as the basis of coins. Its possession has fostered political strength over the centuries, from Alexander to Hitler and from Croesus to President de Gaulle. Its history reflects human psychology.

Markets in Gold

London has had a gold market of sorts for centuries—ever since the merchanting classes began to show their growing commercial strength. The goldsmiths began as processors of gold, gradually becoming holders of gold and, eventually, as we saw in Chapter 2, embryo bankers.

Throughout these developments, they naturally dealt in gold and made a market in gold. But it was hardly the gold market we know today; and between then and now came the century and more of the gold standard and the subsequent gold exchange standard when, for quite different reasons, the London gold market price was also not as free as it has since become.

Uses of Gold

Behind these developments lie the uses to which mankind has put gold: as a form of money; as an adornment; and as an industrial ingredient.

Since gold was first mined about 4000 B.C., it is estimated that some 100,000 tons have been dug out of the ground—mainly in South Africa, California, Alaska, Russia, Canada and Australia. Of this tonnage, about a third is now in official hands as national gold reserves. The rest is in private hands (basically around necks and arms, in mouths, under beds or in banks), in industrial use or simply lost.

Thus the use of gold for private purposes has competed with its use for official monetary purposes. While the first has encouraged an opening up of freer gold markets, the latter has often led to restrictions on the movement of market prices.

From 1815 (the end of the Napoleonic wars) to 1914, the western world was basically on a gold standard or at least Britain, the leading industrial nation, was. This implied that Britain was obliged to pay gold in exchange for its international debts at fixed prices, and that a link existed between its gold reserves and the volume of its internal currency. Other countries such as France, Germany and the United States adopted the gold standard discipline for certain spells. Since 1919 individual nations have moved from the gold standard to a so-called gold exchange standard (under which individual currencies were linked to gold) and, since 1973, to a system only loosely based on gold.

The London gold market has reflected these changes directly. When Britain was on the gold standard, the London gold market price could only move between the statutory buying and selling prices of the Bank of England. The movement in effect reflected changes between sterling and other foreign currencies. The gold market was thus in reality a part of the foreign exchange market, or rather the international market in commercial bills.

Once the gold standard was finally abandoned in 1931, no such official buying and selling prices for gold existed until the United States adopted a gold exchange standard in 1934, under which the U.S. was obliged to buy gold offered to it at $35 an ounce. With this modified arrangement in place, the London gold price was also once more restricted in its potential movement.

In effect, the gold price could hardly drop below $35 an ounce or its sterling equivalent. If it did so, for any length of time, it would pay people to buy gold in London and offer it to the U.S. Treasury at the official price of $35. In addition, the fixed rate of exchange between the U.S. dollar and the pound, which prevailed until 1971, ensured further stability in the sterling price of gold.

London Market

The London gold market as we now know it was opened in 1919 and closed between 1939 and 1954. When it re-opened in the spring of 1954, it quickly re-established itself as the largest in the world.

The reason was simple. The world's largest gold producer, South Africa, arranged to sell the bulk of her output through London, as did Canada, Australia and the United States. In addition, the Soviet Union, the world's second largest producer, used London dealers to sell a large part of her sales. Moreover, the world's central banks also made most of their official gold dealings through the London market. These dealings were originally a matter of re-adjusting the size of national holdings, reflecting the ebb and flow of international trade. But from 1960 onwards, the world's leading central banks deliberately bought and sold gold on the London market as an official pool in attempts to curb speculative movements in the gold price. The Bank of England ran this official consortium.

In fact these attempts to control the gold price eventually failed and in the first half of March 1968, after selling no less than $3,000 million worth of gold in a fortnight in attempts to offset an unprecedented speculative demand for gold, the official Gold Pool gave up the attempt. The Governor of the Bank of England closed the London gold market on March 15 and flew to Washington to meet other central bank governors to consider what to do next. They eventually decided to stop their official interventions in the market, and to create a two-tier system which would accommodate (i) official dealings among central banks, and (ii) free-market dealings. The first maintained the official U.S. price of gold; the second was allowed to reflect private demand.

This was yet a further example of the way in which official uses of gold interfered with, and restricted, what was in effect a private gold market. Thus the London market, which had attracted the bulk of official gold dealings, suffered accordingly. It was closed for just over a fortnight—from March 15 to April 1, 1968. And, not surprisingly, found that the Zurich gold market had stolen a good slice of the world's business in its absence. Middle Eastern and Far Eastern demand had switched to Switzerland and so too had South African supplies, for a variety of reasons, some political, some financial. What was to be a decade and a half of intense rivalry between London and Zurich had begun.

One final move freeing the London market price from undue official restraints was needed; and it came in 1971 when the United States effectively devalued the U.S. dollar and, at the same time, severed its direct link with gold.

How the Market Works

Throughout these remarkable international gyrations, the modern London gold market had continued to operate in much the same way as it did, originally, on September 12, 1919. Rothschild's still house the market and still provide the market's daily chairman. Even the main participants are almost the same, though their ownership has changed over the years: N.M. Rothschild (founded 1804); Bank of Nova Scotia (Mocatta and Goldsmid founded 1684); Deutsche Bank Sharps Pixley (Sharps founded in 1750 and merged with Pixley in 1852); Hong Kong and Shanghai Banking Corporation (Samuel Montagu founded 1853), and Republic National Bank of New York (Johnson Matthey).

Gold price fixing at the offices of N. M. Rothschild & Sons (Colour Chrome Studios)

In 1987 this inner core of members decided to form the London Bullion Market Association and the new structure and membership were agreed in April 1988. Members now total 62. Twelve are accepted as "market-makers". The remaining 50 are classified as "ordinary members". Market-makers are supervised by the Bank of England. Members are drawn from the major gold centres worldwide—including Zurich, Frankfurt, Sydney, Tokyo and New York. The Bank of China is a member.

The five main members meet twice a day (at 10.30 a.m. and 3.00 p.m.) in the portrait-lined room at Rothschild's in New court, a small courtyard in a narrow City street, close to the Bank of England. The portraits of several European monarchs are a daily reminder of Rothschild's early financial history.

This then is where the world's demand for, and supply of, gold comes to a head daily and produces a morning and an afternoon "fixing", the latter specifically geared to North American dealings later in the day. The market in fact continues from 8.00 a.m. to 5.00 p.m., both before and after the "fixing", and continues until 7.30 p.m. in London until the New York "Comex" market opens.

The daily fixing is the price at which the five market members are able to agree they will satisfy the outstanding buying and selling orders for gold. To achieve such an agreed price, the members sit at individual desks around the room. Each member has his own buying and selling orders before him and is in telephonic communication with his office throughout the session. Before and after the fixing all members deal with each other without paying value added tax, provided that the physical delivery of gold is not effected outside the membership.

The chairman from Rothschild's conducts each session and attempts to find a price at which outstanding buying and selling orders can be matched. Each member has a small Union Jack on his desk. So long as the flag remains upright, the dealer is unwilling to agree to the suggested price. When all flags have been lowered, indicating assent, the price is "fixed" and immediately published world-wide.

There are several advantages in channelling orders through the "fixing" process. The spread between buying and selling prices is narrow. The seller is assured of the "fixing" price and the buyer pays a small commission in addition to the "fixing" price. The agreed price at each fixing is based on actual transactions and can be used as such in legal negotiations. The world's central banks use it to value their gold reserves.

London: World Centre

There is now no doubt that London has overtaken Zurich again in the past decade and a half as the world's leading gold transaction and clearing centre. It is also clear that New York is now the leading world centre for gold futures. Several factors have led to this.

Zurich's involvement with gold has come from her traditional role in partly financing and partly supplying refined gold to the Italian gold jewellery trade. The top three (now two) Swiss banks have refineries close to the Italian border and it was natural for them to establish channels for the provision of gold from the producers to the Italian skilled designers and manufacturers. That link still remains and the Swiss banks remain active players on the world gold scene. Physical gold moves in and out of Switzerland as a result and explains Zurich's continuing role as a physical gold transaction centre.

London traditionally was the main outlet for Commonwealth gold and London's role as a leading financial centre fully explained in historical terms the prime role played by the London gold market. Over the last two decades of the twentieth century the emergence of what are now termed "bullion banks" has more than buttressed London's key role.

Briefly, what emerged was a new approach to the financing of new gold mining ventures through project finance and the growing use of derivatives of all kinds (see Chapter 12). "Bullion banking" techniques, developed by leading investment banks, some commercial banks and leading bullion dealers showed how (by borrowing gold from the central banks at low rates of interest and ingenious use of hedging on the gold futures market) new gold projects could be protected from a future decline in the gold price.

This is an over-simplification of a particularly complex operation. But it led to the need for central banks to lend to reliable authorised bullion banks. And, by the facilities offered by the Bank of England, such transactions were centred in London, as were many of the world's "bullion bankers". What the Bank of England offered such banks, through what is known as the London Bullion Clearing, was safe-keeping gold facilities and, most important, individual gold accounts. (The Federal Bank of New York offers such accounts to central banks only.) The Bank of England's facilities meant that the necessary transactions between central banks and bullion banks could be safely undertaken through the authorised London Clearing.

London's Advantages

London's role as the world's largest gold clearing centre and major gold market was thus assured. There were other reasons too:

- London's time zone advantage, coupled with London dealers' subsidiaries in Hong Kong, Sydney, Singapore and New York, the other main trading centres outside Europe.
- The acceptance of London's spot quotation, known as gold "loco-London". This is "for delivery London", enhances the role of London in handling physical gold and ensures that it acts as the clearing centre for the international market.
- London is the only market to publish a Gold LIBOR for one, two, six and twelve months. (See Chapter 10 for an explanation of LIBOR.)

It has always been difficult to assess the turnover in the world's gold markets. Security and thus secrecy have gone hand in hand. London at least has now lifted the veil a little. Starting in 1996 the London Bullion Market Association began to publish monthly turnover based on some of its members. Since then the *daily* total of transactions has moved between 30 and 40 million troy ounces, worth between $10 billion and $13 billion each day. To put this into perspective, London's daily gold turnover is equivalent to twice the annual gold production of South Africa or closely equivalent to the average level of gold holdings of European Union central banks. No other gold market has yet followed London's initiative.

12. Commodity Markets

What They Are

A maritime nation, trading manufactured goods for commodities, attracts markets where such raw materials can be bought and sold. London's markets thus developed as a natural adjunct to trade. They have continued as natural indicators of world prices. And they have spawned a variety of futures markets, which we shall describe in the next chapter.

The commodity markets we are concerned with vary considerably in the way they operate, mainly reflecting the commodities themselves. Some, like furs, tea or feathers, are of varying quality. Others, like copper or tin, can be of standardised quality. Thus some need auction techniques; others simply an open outcry forum.

The main markets can be divided into the following categories:

Exchanges: (for sale of sugar, cocoa, copper, coffee, etc.)—Competitive outcry system with standardised qualities.

Sale Rooms: (for the sale of spices, nuts, fibres, etc.)—Deals between agents, representing buyers and sellers.

Auctions: (for the sale of tea, furs, etc.)—Competitive bidding, after examination.

This list would not be complete unless trading in oil were also included though it hardly fits into these categories. Oil, however, as the most heavily traded cash commodity in the world, has not escaped the City's attention, as we shall see in the next chapter on derivatives.

How They Work

It is the exchanges, that is the world markets for "hard" and "soft" commodities, that we shall be primarily concerned with in this chap-

95

ter. The "hard" commodities include the non-ferrous metals such as lead, tin, zinc and copper, and the "soft" commodities coffee, cocoa and sugar. The hard commodities are administered by the London Metal Exchange and the soft commodities by the London Commodity Exchange, now part of LIFFE.

The main "hard" and "soft" commodities are traded in what are known as "rings". The dealers sit in an arranged circle and during the individual sessions bid verbally between each other. Hence the description of an open "outcry" system. Those seated around the ring, who are enabled to deal, are representatives of ring-dealing firms. Many are based overseas. Although the "outcry" system has been maintained at the basic sessions, these exchanges have not ignored the technological advances that have been made. Outcry and electronic systems exist side by side.

At the London Metal Exchange, clerks man the telephones immediately behind the ring, passing on the latest market information, receiving new market orders and transmitting the latest deals and prices. In addition inter-office trading also takes place with the use of electronic equipment. (Dealings by screen are not used.) The offices in turn will be in telephone, fax or telex communication with business contacts world-wide.

These official sessions undertake three basic operations:

- They enable commodities to be bought and sold, under guaranteed conditions.
- They enable world price quotations to be established in an open market place.
- They offer hedging facilities—means of protection against sharp changes in prices, which we shall be exploring more closely in the next chapter.

A distinction has to be made between the metals and the soft commodities. Whereas deals in copper, zinc, lead, aluminium and nickel are traded on a daily basis up to 15 or 27 months ahead, depending on the metal, others offer longer-term futures. Secondly, while there is an obligation on members to acquire or deliver physical *metal* on the specified date of a contract, no similar obligation attaches to other commodities.

These distinctions basically reflect the rules and regulations of the different associations governing commodity dealings in the Square Mile. It is necessary, therefore, to outline separately the individual roles played by the various bodies involved.

London Metal Exchange　The Exchange has its own Board of Directors and operates its daily metal markets at 56, Leadenhall Street. These operate between 11.45 a.m. and 1.30 p.m. and, in the afternoon, between 3.20 p.m. and 5.00 p.m.

Each of the eight metals (copper, zinc, lead, aluminium, aluminium alloy, nickel, silver and tin) is allotted two trading sessions of five minutes each, in the morning and afternoon. What are known as "kerb" dealings in all the metals take place for twenty minutes after the morning and afternoon sessions.

The "official" prices for prompt and forward delivery are monitored by a quotations committee and announced after the morning session. These prices are used by producer countries and the majority of the world's industry for pricing raw materials.

There are 14 ring dealing members at present. Of these, well over half are owned or partly owned by overseas companies. They have an obligation to receive or deliver physical metal, according to contract, unless the transaction has been "squared" by a corresponding contract the other way. The physical deliveries are made by the presentation of warrants at LME registered warehouses in the U.K., Europe, Singapore, Japan and the USA.

London Commodity Exchange (LCE)   This is the centre for "soft" commodities—cocoa, robusta coffee, raw and white sugar—as well as agricultural commodities and BIFFEX (shipping freight rate index). LCE is responsible for the futures and traded options markets in these commodities as well as administration, management and communications.

IPE   The IPE is Europe's leading energy futures and options exchange, and the second largest in the world. The IPE provides a highly regulated marketplace where industry participants can manage their exposure to highly volatile energy prices. Incorporated in 1980, the IPE lists three main energy contracts: Brent Crude features and options, Gas Oil futures and options, and Natural Gas futures. The IPE is a member owned exchange, and clients can access the market either by becoming a Member or by using the broking services available from Members. Trades are cleared by the London Clearing House, which guarantees contract performance.

London Clearing House   This organisation enables the various markets to operate successfully. Its primary role is to guarantee contract performance by becoming the central counterparty to all contracts registered in the names of its clearing members. This enables clearing members to settle their obligations without any reference to the other

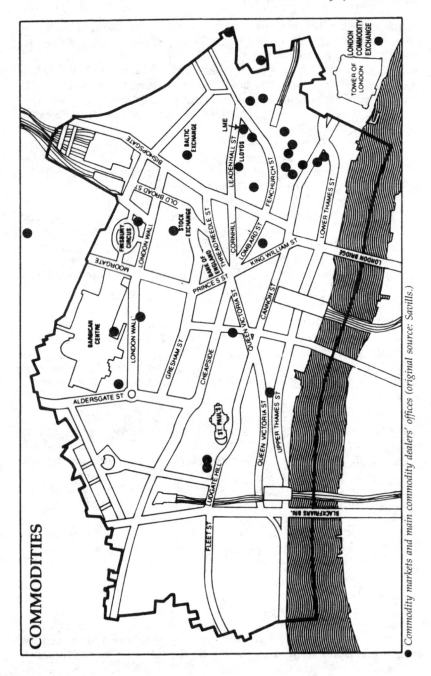

Commodity markets and main commodity dealers' offices (original source: Savills.)

original contracting parties and thus provide a basic assurance to clearing members that individual obligations will be fulfilled.

LCH is one of the largest global clearing houses, clearing a broad range of financial futures or options, equities, metals, soft commodities and energy products traded on four London recognised investment exchanges—London International Financial Futures Exchange (LIFFE), London International Petroleum Exchange (IPE), London Metal Exchange (LME) and Tradepoint Stock Exchange (Tradepoint).

OM London Exchange   Finally, we need to include the description of a relatively recent market. Though it bases itself on securities, not commodities, it concentrates on derivatives, which we tackle in the next chapter, and arranges its own clearing system. Known as the OM London Exchange, the London Securities and Derivatives Exchange is one of the recognised Investment Exchanges in the U.K. and, as such, is regulated by the FSA. It offers a fully electronic market-place—with the "Click" trading system permitting access for all members and total anonymity for all users of the market. The exchange has an integrated clearing house which ensures the integrity of each trade entered into by the exchange's members, and has the backing of a parent company guarantee to the value of £115 million.

Although originally established in 1989 as the London arm of the Swedish company, OM Gruppen AB, it provides flexible and cost-effective exposure to the U.K. and Swedish stock markets.

Basic Facilities   It is time to remind ourselves what these different organisations are providing for customers. Both producers and consumers of commodities are given certain basic facilities in the London markets:

- Markets for arranging sales and purchases of individual commodities.
- World spot and futures prices on a daily basis.
- A choice between "exchange traded products" (*i.e.* standardised contracts) and "over the counter (OTC) products" (*i.e.* customised contracts).
- Clearing arrangements and trading guarantees.
- Futures and option facilities.

How the futures markets, and derivatives generally, work now needs to be considered separately, in a chapter of its own.

13. Derivatives, Futures, Options, . . .

Prices in free markets can go up and down. This is just as true of currencies, securities, bonds and other financial instruments, as it is of second-hand cars, apples or copper. In the past decade and a half, both exchange rates and interest rates have been more volatile than at any time since the Second World War. Commodity prices too have hardly been stable.

Not surprisingly, the City's markets, like their counterparts in Chicago and New York, have begun to provide (or in some cases, improve) ways of reducing the risks which accompany such gyrations. They have done this by the development of facilities such as forward markets, futures markets and option markets, now known generally as derivative markets.

In some cases, these markets have simply revived old pre-war habits such as in the forward exchange markets and the security option markets. In others, new facilities have been introduced, especially in the futures markets in financial instruments such as securities, currencies and the like. And it is here that a new exciting industry, "risk management", has been spawned and where, as Baring's merchant bank found, some frightening new dangers lurk too.

What They Do

Basically these markets offer ways of modifying future or existing risks. They also provide opportunities for outright speculation. The choice is up to the customer, but both functions are needed to give the depth of turnover such markets need.

The first step in understanding what they offer is to differentiate between forward markets, futures markets and option markets.

Forward Markets

These basically operate in the foreign exchange and commodity markets. They offer contracts between one trader and another, promising to buy or sell a specified volume of a commodity or a currency on a certain date. They enable a trader who has an obligation to give or receive an agreed amount (of a commodity or currency) on a future date to protect himself against a fluctuation in the price of that commodity or currency in the interim.

The essential characteristics of a forward contract are: (i) it is undertaken for any required volume, (ii) the commodity or currency is expected to be delivered, (iii) the contract cannot be transferred or sold to second or third parties (*i.e.* it cannot be "traded"), (iv) the contract need not be published.

Futures Markets Like forward markets, they offer a place where contracts are arranged between traders, promising to deliver an agreed amount of a commodity, security or currency on an agreed date, at a price. They offer the same protection as a forward contract.

The essential characteristics of a futures market, in contrast to a forward market are: (i) the contracts are standardised, (ii) business is open and prices published, (iii) the contracts can thus be traded (*i.e.* the obligations can be subsequently bought and sold), (iv) dealings are usually organised by a clearing house, providing protection to the participants.

The main contracts in the futures markets concern securities, currencies and commodities.

Option Markets These too concern contracts for future settlement, but the emphasis is on a *right*, which the holder of the option may exercise if he wishes, to buy or sell a commodity, security or currency, not an *obligation* as in the case of forward or futures markets. Warrants, usually attached to securities, are in effect longer-term options.

Options have a terminology of their own. A "call" option is a right to *buy* and a "put" option is a right to *sell*. The future price at which the option can be taken is called the "strike price".

Option markets are not new. But *traded* option markets on which the rights to buy or sell can be passed on to others are a more recent development.

The main contracts in the option markets concern securities and currencies.

Where They Are

The origin of today's futures markets was probably in Antwerp (in the sixteenth century), followed by Amsterdam (in the seventeenth century) and Chicago (in the nineteenth century). Options were developed in London in the nineteenth century. More recent developments have emerged, again, from Chicago and, subsequently, from New York, London, Amsterdam, Sydney, Philadelphia, Paris, Hong Kong, Singapore, Tokyo and Bermuda.

The main innovation has, of course, been in financial derivatives of all kinds, initially in Chicago, more recently, and vigorously, in London. Let one of London's experts, Anthony Belchambers of the Futures and Options Association, set the recent scene:

"What is new is the application of futures to the raw material of the financial world, namely, money. This had led to a world-wide proliferation of financial exchanges, new generation products and, indeed, customers . . . Today, there are over 70 derivative exchanges trading, mainly financial derivatives, in 30 different locations around the world capturing between them 95 per cent of the world's market capitalisation and most of the world's tradeable commodities."

The long-established Chicago exchanges—the Chicago Board of Trade and the Chicago Mercantile Exchange—were the first to introduce financial futures in the 1970s. London followed with its own new exchange, LIFFE, in 1982. Ten years later LIFFE's physical turnover (not by value) exceeded that in Chicago for the first time. Although the Chicago exchanges are ahead of LIFFE in terms of the value of turnover, LIFFE is the first in Europe, third in the world and offers a greater diversity of financial and commodity contracts than either Chicago or New York.

The various markets do not operate from one spot in London, but are scattered over different sections of the Square Mile. Let me therefore sum up who does what, where:

● *The London International Financial Futures and Options Exchange* (LIFFE) offers futures and options trading on U.K., German, Italian and Japanese Government bonds, and Sterling, Euro, U.S. Dollar, Deutschmark, Swiss Franc, yen and Italian Lira short-term interest rates, spanning seven different currencies. In addition, LIFFE also offers futures and options on U.K. stock indices and 72 individual equity options.

102

- *London Commodity Exchange* (LCE) now part 2 LIFFE, offers commodity futures and traded options contracts in cocoa, coffee, sugar, grain, potatoes and BIFFEX.
- *The London Stock Exchange* offers equity and index options.
- *London Metal Exchange* (LME) offers commodity hedging contracts.
- *International Petroleum Exchange* (IPE) offers futures contracts in Brent crude oil, gas oil, and unleaded gasoline as well as options contracts in Brent crude oil and gas oil.
- *London Foreign Exchange Market* offers forward currency contracts.
- *International banks* in London offer customised currency option contracts.
- *The OMLX exchange* lists standardised futures and options contracts on the Swedish OMX stock index and individual Swedish equities which are among the most liquid and highly traded derivatives in Europe. It also offers clearing services for a range of Swedish bond and interest rate derivatives which are traded interbank.
- *London Clearing House* (LCH) provides clearing and guarantee facilities for the London derivative markets, apart from the OMLX exchange, as well as for other City markets (see Chapter 12).

How They Work

Since forward, futures and option markets are available in several different spots and cover several different instruments, it is easier to explain how they work by choosing a typical example in each market.

1. Forward Contracts in Foreign Exchange Foreign exchange risks have been rising rapidly over the past decade and a half as the fixed exchange rate regime set up at Bretton Woods in 1946 gradually broke down under the combined assault of inflation, oil price decisions, fluctuating interest rates and currency doubts.

This has led to a bigger turnover in the *forward exchange markets* as big corporations, increasingly conscious of their exposure to exchange rate risks, arising from their foreign operations, have felt the need for additional protection.

The risks are of different kinds:

(i) An exporter sells large quantities of his goods to a French buyer at today's prices, but will not be paid in French francs until delivery in three months time. By then the exchange rate may have moved decisively upwards or downwards.

(ii) An importer contracts to buy, say, 5,000 Japanese cars over the next six months and agrees to pay in six months time at *current* Japanese prices. If the pound declines in value over the following six months, he will have to pay more in pounds to meet the Japanese cost of the cars.

In each case, one way to offset, or at least limit, the risk arising from a change in the exchange rate is to buy or sell (depending on the kind of risk he is running) an equivalent amount of foreign currency three or six months ahead. The purchase or sale of the foreign exchange is meant to match the outstanding obligation and is undertaken for forward delivery at an agreed future date at today's exchange rate, with a so-called forward premium. The forward premium is the price paid for protection. It is based on a number of factors, primarily the difference in interest rates between the two countries concerned, but also a variety of political and economic factors likely to affect the demand for and supply of the two currencies.

The interest rate differential is not difficult to understand. A bank with £1,000 in London wishing to exchange it into dollars in three months time, is faced with a choice: it can leave it in London, earning the London rate of interest of, say, 11 per cent, and then switch it into dollars in three months time or switch it into dollars now (at the current rate of exchange) and earn, say, 8 per cent in New York. The forward exchange rate available will reflect this difference in interest rates as well as other factors.

2. Option Contracts in Securities   Options are remarkably flexible in their application. When used in conjunction with securities, they can help to protect an existing holding of shares against a marked drop in share prices; to protect an investor in a variety of other ways; or simply to encourage a speculative venture.

It is useful to repeat exactly what the different options imply. "Call" options give the right to buy shares at a previously agreed price (to help the memory think of them as "calling" the shares from their original owner). "Put" options provide a facility to sell shares at an agreed price ("putting" them on to a new owner).

Let us take an example of each.

A shareholder owning 1,000 shares in ICI may fear that the share price is likely to fall, but may not wish to sell his shares. The option market will allow him to buy a "put" option, that is the right to sell his shares at an agreed price (the prices available are in specified steps). If the price goes down as he expects, he can *either* take up the option to sell the shares at the chosen price (*i.e.* at a higher price than in the depressed market) or he can sell the "put" option, again at a profit. The reason for the profit on the "put" option is that "put" options rise in value as prices decline, whereas "call" options do the opposite (*i.e.* they rise when share prices rise). If the shares had risen, his shares would be worth more and he would simply allow the "put" option to lapse, having paid a small premium for protection against a fall.

Take another example, the case of an investor who expects a share price to go up before he has the resources to buy in the market. In these circumstances, he can buy a "call" option, which will allow him the right to buy his shares at an agreed price in the future. If the price rises, so does the value of his options. He then has a choice depending on circumstances. He can take up his option and buy the shares at the favourable price (*i.e.* lower than the increased one in the market) *or* he can sell the options at their higher value.

One point worth grasping about options is the effect of "gearing", a term we have already met in the case of investment trusts. Since an option costs only a fraction of the price of a share and since option prices tend to move in line with share prices, the *percentage* changes in option prices are inevitably greater than in the underlying share prices. It means that big profits *and big losses* can quickly be realised, unless the investor is clear what he is doing.

The conclusion to be drawn is simple: before plunging into the option market, get a wet towel, a good adviser and ask yourself these questions (as the Stock Exchange itself advises) at the outset:

● What is my purpose: protection or speculation?
● How much capital can I afford to risk?
● How long should I wait before deciding to act during the period of an option?

3. Options on Futures In the case of commodities it is already possible to take out options on certain commodity futures such as cocoa, coffee and raw sugar. Similar developments were once thought likely in the currency field, though the existence of a high-turnover foreign exchange market, with built-in forward transactions for the main currencies, might inhibit these developments.

4. Options in Currencies The option markets in currencies began as "customised" foreign exchange currency options, a modified facility offered to individual customers by the big international banks through the foreign exchange market. They were clearly attractive. Corporate customers were getting what amounted to a personal service, options being written for sums and dates which exactly matched the customer's needs. The banks who wrote such specialised options, however, naturally saw it differently, since these and other option operations were unlikely to match and this often exposed the banks to unwanted risks. These anxieties naturally increased the interest in the development of *"traded"* (standardised) foreign currency options first in Philadelphia, and then for a time in London.

5. Futures Contracts in Commodities and Securities   These contracts began in commodities and have been extended to securities, currencies and shipping freights. In each case the aims of operators are the same: to protect an existing situation against any adverse future change in prices or to speculate.

The positions that need protection vary considerably:

- A manufacturer who has ordered raw materials in advance at agreed prices fears a drop in prices.
- A manufacturer who has agreed to supply products at fixed prices for future delivery, fears a rise in prices.
- A ship-owner who has chartered his vessels at a fixed time charter rate for the next six months, fears a fall in prices.
- An importer who needs to make an agreed payment in dollars in future, fears a drop in the value of his own currency.
- A company holding stocks of unsold products or materials, fears a drop in prices.
- An investor intending to invest £1 in a fixed-interest security in two months time, fears a drop in interest rates (and a rise in security prices).

In each case a drop (or rise) in commodity prices, security prices, currency values or interest rates could lead to a future loss. In some cases the precise nature of the risk is known, because of the details of a contract. In others, the exact size of the risk is not known. A futures market helps to reduce the risk and we now need to see how it is done.

We can take two different, though simple, examples. In the first case (Example A), a manufacturer has bought stocks of raw material and fears that prices will fall. In the second case (Example B), a corporate Treasurer has a million dollars to invest two months ahead. In the first example the risk is covered by the sale of futures (this is known as a *short* hedge). In the second example, it is covered by the purchase of futures (a *long* hedge).

Example A The manufacturer's normal transactions are shown under the "physical market" column in the table below. His subsequent transactions in the futures market, to protect himself against loss, arising from a fall in prices, are shown in the "futures market" column:

	Physical Market	**Futures Market**
March 1	Makes a fixed contract to buy 1,000 tonnes of cocoa at £1,500 per tonne.	Sells 1,000 tonnes of cocoa at £1,510 for delivery in June.
June 1	Sells 1,000 tonnes of cocoa at £1,490.	Buys 1,000 tonnes of cocoa at £1,490 for the spot month (*i.e.* June).
	Loss of £10,000	*Profit of £20,000*

Example B A corporate Treasurer, knowing he will have $1 million to invest in fixed-interest deposits in two months time, wishes to avoid receiving less because of an expected fall in interest rates. So he undertakes the futures contracts shown in the second column:

	Cash Market	**Futures Market**
January 1	Treasurer will have $1 million to invest on March 1. Current interest rate is 10% pa on Euro-dollar deposit.	Buys a March 3-month Euro-dollar deposit futures contract at 90, reflecting interest rate of 10% pa.
March 1	Treasurer invests $1 million in 3-month deposit at 8% pa.	Sells a March 3-month Euro-dollar futures contract at 92, reflecting interest rate of 8% pa.
	Notional Loss: $5,000	*Gain: $5,000*

A New Market

It is time to sketch in briefly, therefore, what direction recent uses of these essentially simple tools has taken. What is now known as a global derivative market has created a whole new range of financial activities as well as dramatic new pitfalls.

The word derivative, meaning an instrument derived from an asset such as fuel, food, metal or money, has naturally become all-embracing and is not always used in the same way. Originally (and to some extent this still applies) it embraced forwards, futures, options and warrants, which we described earlier. Swaps too, which we met in Chapter 10, and are basically agreements to exchange cash flows relating to interest rate or exchange rate differences, are now included.

In addition derivatives can be based on products traded under the rules of an exchange (*i.e.* standardised contracts) or "over the counter" (*i.e.* customised contracts). The latter (*i.e.* OTC) are often the main kind of derivatives recognised in the United States. So beware how people (and above all statistics) are using the word.

To realise just what has been created in little more than two decades, consider the size of the derivative markets. In 1993 the world's seventy odd derivative exchanges between them traded over a billion individual contracts for the first time and volume has continued to rise.

Yet that figure is dwarfed by the volume of business undertaken "over the counter". The International Swaps and Derivatives Association estimates that world-wide turnover in OTC derivatives and swaps at the beginning of 1998 had reached close on $30 trillion of notional capital. Interest rate swaps accounted for the largest slice.

The Risks

Just as the original modest futures or option deals from which this vast new industry began could offer either increased protection or enhanced risks, so can the much larger and far more sophisticated instruments in use today. But the stakes are rather higher, as an increasing number of industrial and financial clients can verify. It became increasingly clear to the more enterprising bankers, analysts and dealers that financial futures and options could, with some dexterity, be transformed into highly complex instruments specifically designed for individual corporations. "Risk management" as a technique was overnight transformed into a new industry. Yet what could, in the right hands, be used as protection against market fluctuations and dangers, could equally, in the wrong hands or with the wrong advice, actually double and treble the risks.

Hedge Funds

Not only were derivatives being designed for individual corporations and investors, but they soon attracted the attention of investment funds too. So-called "hedge funds" were the outcome. These are basically funds that are deliberately structured to be exempt from investor protection requirements and pursue highly flexible investment strategies, such as taking long and short positions (*i.e.* having deliberate surpluses or shortages of, say, equities or currencies) and then increasing those positions (known as gearing, which we discussed in Chapter 5). Trading in derivatives was one way of achieving such enhanced results—whether profits or losses. Speculation, not protection, became the main objective. At present there are some 1,200 hedge funds with

LIFFE (London International Financial Futures and Options Exchange

LIFFE is one of Europe's premier financial derivatives exchanges. It offers the ability to hedge and trade across the world's broadest range of products and is the only exchange in the world to offer futures and option contracts on all the following products: financial (currency and interest rates), equity indices, equities and commodities.

LIFFE, established in 1982, has recently changed its structure and its market mechanism to reflect its expansion and its need to maintain its lead in Europe. Its share structure has been streamlined to one class of Ordinary share and traders are now subscription-based and not dependent on permits. It has thus severed the original link between shareholding and the right to trade.

Until recently, LIFFE was the most colourful of the City's "outcry" markets, its trading floor providing television with its essential City action image. That still continues and may for some time, but increasingly the market will be geared to electronic trading on screens alone.

While the outcry system lasts, its deals are done in a more orderly fashion than a visitor would guess:

● An order to buy or sell a futures or options contract is telephoned from a trader's office to its booth on the trading floor. This is given by *a yellow-jacketed* runner to a trader.
● The trader, in a *scarlet jacket*, gives his order in the appropriate "pit" on the floor of the exchange by open outcry and the use of hand signals. (Each contract has its own "pit".)
● Details of the deal are put on an order slip and confirmed with the customer.
● Every trade is reported by a pit observer and the information keyed into the Price Reporting System.

This open outcry system is already supplemented by screen-based trading. In addition a new electronic system, called *LIFFE CONNECT*, has been installed. Several contracts have already been transferred from "open outcry" to electronic and, like the Stock Exchange (see Chapter 4), are now order-driven rather than quote-driven. The prices shown on the new system's screen will thus represent firm buy and sell orders instead of indicative quotes. This is plainly the way of the future world-wide.

around $120 billion under management. Some take big risks; some do not.

The outcome was not difficult to guess. Individuals, corporations and institutions were soon recording unexpectedly large losses from unfortunate participations in both derivative trading and in hedge funds. The largest and most spectacular failure of a hedge fund was that of Long Term Capital Management in 1998, needing a £2 billion bailout. In derivatives alone, a Japanese oil company lost $1.5 billion trading in currency. Britain's oldest merchant bank, Baring's, crashed overnight. Small British local authorities recorded losses of £100 million in swap transactions. Orange County, with 25 per cent of its assets in derivatives and a subsequent loss of some $1.5 billion, was only the first of several American local administrations to realise the dangers of derivatives. Even an Indian tribe invested close on $5 million in mortgage derivatives and lost most of it. The list, and the consequent legal cases, is lengthening daily.

Prospects

The world's regulators are, not surprisingly, beginning to ask some serious questions. Do hedge funds need regulating and should they be bailed out if they fail? Could derivative trading, if unchecked, undermine not only individuals and corporations, but currencies, major stock markets and crucial financial institutions? Though customers must look after themselves, innocent by-standers may be at risk too. At present official attention is directed towards: (i) requiring more regular information from participants about their hedged positions; (ii) ensuring that existing regulations are monitored; and (iii) tightening up international capital requirements of participants. The world's central banks, through the Bank for International Settlements, have already initiated such a regular reporting and monitoring operation.

14. Baltic Exchange

London has been a trading port for centuries, at least since the Romans confirmed it as a major crossing point on the Thames. Goods were naturally exchanged, and needed to be financed and insured. And the river, and the nearby estuary, brought ships.

So the proximity of the Baltic Exchange, Lloyd's Register of Shipping and the General Council of British Shipping, within a stone's throw of Lloyd's, hosts of foreign banks and London's commodity markets, is hardly a chance development. Shipping remains at the centre of the City's commercial activities.

What it Does

The place where this is most manifest is the trading floor of the Baltic Exchange in St Mary Axe. This is where the world's traders come to find a ship for their goods or goods for their ships; where second-hand ships are bought and sold; and where air freight and spare aircraft capacity are married together.

The Baltic was for many years primarily concerned with tramp shipping, that is with vessels which were not on scheduled services and were therefore available for hire. It is now basically concerned with purpose-built bulk carriers of all kinds—dry cargo, oil tankers, multi-deck vessels, roll-on roll-off ships for cars, trucks, etc. But the market's principle remains the same. The Exchange brings together, directly or indirectly, the owners or operators of ships available for hire and charterers or hirers who wish to use them to take goods between agreed destinations at mutually agreed prices. These agreements are usually made voyage by voyage (or series of voyages) or over specified periods of time.

Thus firms with goods or commodities to shift round the world, either single cargoes or regularly, will use the Baltic to discuss what ships are available. Coal producers and their shippers will go there to find ships to transport coal from Hampton Roads in the U.S. to South Japan. Equally shippers of grain will look for vessels to ship it from the U.S. Gulf to Rotterdam.

What it is

The Baltic Exchange is an organisation providing its members with premises, facilities and agreed rules of conduct to enable them to undertake shipping, commodity and other related activities. Just like the Stock Exchange and Lloyd's, its origins lie in the coffee houses of the seventeenth century, where the ships' captains and merchants met to arrange cargoes or ships.

Two particular coffee houses attracted the shipping fraternity, the Jerusalem Coffee House and the Virginia and Maryland Coffee House. The latter subsequently became known as the Virginia and Baltic to reflect the two areas of the world bringing most business. After further expansion the "Baltic" emerged in 1810, produced "Baltic Club" regulations in 1823 and built its previous trading floor, finally damaged by the IRA in 1992, in 1903. The present Exchange opened in 1995, and remained in St Mary Axe.

The Baltic is now made up of over 700 corporate members, with 1500 individual members of some 45 different nationalities. Some members are chartering agents representing merchants who have cargoes to move round the world. Others are owners' brokers, representing the shipowners. In other cases the merchants and shipowners may be members themselves. Some company members will have both owners' brokers as well as chartering agents under the same roof.

The Baltic International Freight Futures Market (BIFFEX), trading dry bulk cargo freight futures, which opened in 1985, is based on the Baltic Freight Index (BFI) published daily by the Baltic Exchange. The BFI shows the weighted average freight rate level and weighted average trip time charter hire level each day in the dry bulk cargo shipping market.

The Exchange also trades a range of other indices.

Apart from providing a forum for the conduct of international shipping business, the Baltic Exchange has a strict code of ethics, regulates members and mediates in disputes. The motto of the Baltic is "Our word, our bond".

How it Works

Thousands of vessels are at this moment plying the world's oceans. Many have no idea, on arrival at their destination, where they will go

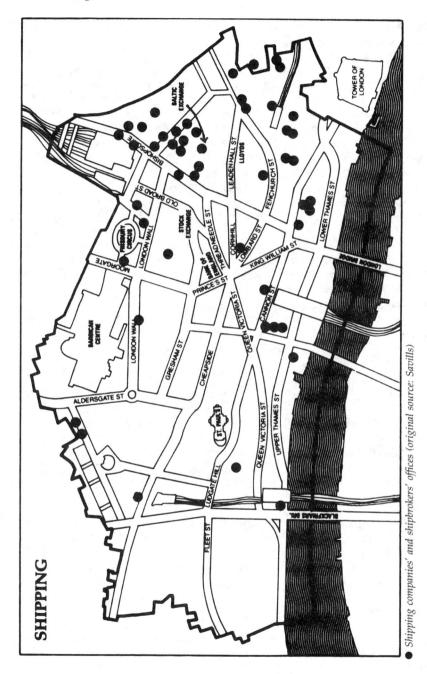

• *Shipping companies' and shipbrokers' offices (original source: Savills)*

next. More often than not, that decision is being decided for them on the Baltic or in one of the offices nearby.

Why the delay, you may ask. The truth is that shipping is fraught with obstacles, both God- and man-made. If a ship is delayed for an hour or a day, that is going to cost someone money somewhere. So it is clearly better to delay final decisions on the next movement of a ship until it is clear that it is able—and free—to go there. The delay, however, simply makes the Baltic more essential than ever. (Or is it simply that because the Baltic exists, the delay in fixing the next leg of a tramp ship's journey is possible?)

As, say, a vessel sails towards Tokyo (or Sydney or Rio de Janeiro), the owners, or their brokers, will be moving on to the floor of the Baltic to secure the next round of business—from Tokyo to where? So will the brokers of other shipowners with ships bound for Tokyo.

At the same time Japanese steel mills may have cargoes they want moved from Tokyo to Los Angeles or Melbourne. Car manufacturers will have regular export shipments to arrange. Much of this information can be circulated by telephone, telex or printed circular. But the face-to-face meeting on the Baltic can also be crucial.

The reason is that some of the details, relating to either cargoes or ships, are highly competitive with other ships and cargoes. So the seeking our of the half dozen likely brokers on the floor and the beginnings of the next essential steps, offers and counter-offers, are often done personally.

Once details have been exchanged between one broker and another, an "indication" is given of the kind of deal contemplated, but it is left to the two principals, the owners, to begin to specify details of a "firm offer" and a "firm counter-offer".

These will contain details of cargoes and ships (fuel consumption, speed, freight charges, when the vessel is available, etc.: the list seems endless) and eventually lead to the drawing up of what is known as a "charterparty" (from the Latin *carta partita*, "divided paper", indicating the two parts of such an agreement). Once agreement is reached, the ship concerned is "fixed".

These "fixtures" often begin on the floor of the Baltic, but rarely are all negotiations concluded there. So, like other City markets, a combination of an open market-place, electronic and telephonic communications and administrative back-up produce the international business the Exchange depends upon.

International Flavour

The essential element remains the presence of so many foreign shipowners and merchants (or their agents or brokers) in the Square Mile.

The British merchant fleet is now a more modest proportion of the world's total, but the agents and brokers of the bigger shipowning nations (whether traditional, new or simply flags of convenience) continue to have a presence in London.

Fewer than 10 per cent of the deals initiated or negotiated on the Baltic involve a British shipowner, importer, exporter or even crew. Yet up to 50 per cent of all dry cargo business "fixed" on the world's open markets will be done by a Baltic member. And over 50 per cent of the sales of ships negotiated world-wide on the open market will also be arranged through a Baltic member.

Ship broking is also conducted in other trade centres such as New York, Oslo, Tokyo, Hamburg, Rotterdam, Paris and Brussels. But in virtually every case, turnover is dominated by national, rather than international, requirements. London still manages to attract the bulk of the international business. Neither Tokyo nor New York are open for business at the same time; yet, because of London's time zone, both can and do manage to conduct business with London at each end of the day. And, cementing these international relationships, many of the Baltic's corporate members have their headquarters outside the U.K. The international flavour of the Baltic Exchange is reflected in the invisible export earnings of its members, producing currently close to £316 million per annum for the U.K. balance of payments.

15. What The City Is

We began this small book with a brief outline of where and how the different City specialisations had developed and we summarised what the City of London did as a whole. Individual chapters have tried to explain how each sector works. In this penultimate chapter, we will attempt to sum up the City's main characteristics and to assess what kind of a financial centre the City now is.

Three main features seem to stand out:

- While servicing the British economy, London concentrates on *international* financial services.
- London offers a *wider variety* of services than other comparable financial centres.
- London is basically a *wholesale* centre in international finance, attracting deposits and business from other centres.

International Services

London's foreign earnings are now well documented. At the last official count, what are known as invisible earnings from Britain's financial services (they include the direct earnings from services to foreigners as well as the return on overseas investments) amounted to £15,605 million net in 1997. The details are shown in the table on page 118.

These are large figures by any standards, but they do not bring out how London, say, compares with New York, Zurich, Paris, Tokyo, etc. To do this, we need to look at each sector of the City separately.

(a) Banking London is running ahead of Tokyo in the proportion of international banking transactions it undertakes. Latest figures (end 1997):

	%
London	19
Tokyo	12
New York	9
Paris	8
Frankfurt	7

(Source: *Bank for International Settlements*)

(b) Foreign Banks   There are now 556 foreign banks represented in London, compared with about 287 in New York, 123 in Paris, 231 in Frankfurt and 101 in Tokyo. There are more American banks in London than in New York.

The establishment of the European Bank for Reconstruction and Development in London, with some 40 countries as shareholders, consolidated London's pre-eminence.

(c) Foreign Exchange   We referred to the size of the turnover in London's foreign exchange market earlier and put it at some $637 billion a day, or some 32 per cent of the world's turnover. How does this compare with other world centres? The Bank of England, U.S. Federal Reserve and the Bank of Japan have made these estimates

	$bn
London	637
New York	351
Tokyo	149
Singapore	139
Frankfurt	94
Zurich	82
Hong Kong	79

(d) Insurance   Since so many countries insist on undertaking their own insurance and since domestic insurance is naturally undertaken by domestic firms in some of the largest markets, such as West Germany and the U.S., international business need to be assessed separately. The London insurance market (Lloyd's and the companies) maintains the largest share of international business in marine (with Tokyo in second place) and in aviation (with New York in second place).

(e) Gold   The turnover of the London gold market is reported to be $30 billion *daily*, ahead of any other centre.
(*Note*: In the case of *gold futures*, the New York COMEX exchange still dominates world transactions.)

City of London's Foreign Earnings[1] 1946–1997

	1946[2] £m	1956[3] £m	1963[4] £m	1965[5] £m	1968 £m	1987 £m	1992 £m	1997 £m
Banks	5–10	25–30	45–50	82.5	67	1,321	2,487	7,745
Insurance	20–25	70	85	81	198	4,440	3,979	7,417
Commodity Trading	5–10	25–30	20–25	80–90	57	—	—	—
Brokerage	10	15–20	20–25	30–35	22	—	—	—
Pension Funds	—	—	—	—	5	695	1,486	2,129
Securities dealers	—	—	—	—	—	1,266	1,147	2,701
Unit Trusts	—	—	—	—	2	219	425	972
Investment Trusts	—	—	—	—	35	170	263	367
Futures and options dealers	—	—	—	—	—	122	279	323
Money market brokers	—	—	—	—	—	59	92	208
Baltic Exchange	—	—	—	—	33	227	300	316
Lloyd's Register of Shipping	—	—	—	—	—	22	39	47
Fund Managers	—	—	—	—	—	—	282	440
Non-specified institutions	—	—	—	—	—	1,329	1,266	2,522
TOTAL	40–55	135–150	170–185	250–290	419	9,870	12,045	25,187

[1] Including Edinburgh
[2] Unofficial estimates by William M. Clarke, *The City in the World Economy*, 1965.
[3] *ibid.*
[4] *ibid.*
[5] From *Britain's Invisible Earnings* (report of the Committee on Invisible Exports, London, 1968)
Source: British Invisibles (B.I.)

(f) Stock Exchange Turnover In terms of domestic turnover the London Stock Exchange ranks fourth, below Tokyo (and Osaka) and New York. If, however, turnover in foreign equities is taken as the measuring rod, London's global share in 1997 was 58 per cent, compared with 24 per cent in New York and about 3 per cent in Tokyo, Paris and Frankfurt combined.

(g) International Equity Listings If the number of foreign company listings is compared, London is the leading centre for equities:

London	526
New York	356
Frankfurt	229
Paris	193

(Source: *London Stock Exchange*)

(h) Euro-currency and Eurobond Markets For a time London took the lion's share of the world's Euro-currency market, largely because the market had developed there. It is still marginally ahead of Tokyo on international banking transactions (see paragraph (a) above). As for Eurobond business, some 60 per cent of primary issues have taken place in London in recent years. Most Euro-dollar, Euro-yen, Canadian dollar and Australian dollar Eurobonds are issued out of London. In the case of the secondary market in international bonds, London claims up to 70 per cent.

(i) Fund Management Both London and Edinburgh are acting as fund managers for domestic and international investments. U.K.-based fund managers currently have over \$1,800 billion of funds under management. London claims over three quarters of foreign institutional funds managed in Europe and the bulk of U.S. pension funds managed outside the U.S.

(j) Derivatives Turnover on LIFFE is now the biggest in Europe and third in the world. London accounts for the largest share of the world's "over the counter" derivative turnover.

(k) Shipping The Baltic Exchange claims that London accounts for between a half and two thirds of international shipping freight "fixtures" relating to dry cargo, and about 50 per cent of the market for sale and purchase of ships world-wide. Lloyd's Register of Shipping is the world's premier ship classification society. London is also a global centre for shipping finance. Half of the world's leading ship finance banks have offices in London.

Variety of Services

Both the individual chapters and the above assessment of London's international services bring out the wide variety of different services available to foreign customers. Basically, London is offering banking and investment services, insurance and re-insurance, commodity dealings, derivative trading, shipping transactions and accountancy and legal advice on a world-wide basis.

This stands in contrast to other international centres which tend to concentrate on a narrower range of services. New York, for example, is strong on banking, investment, insurance and professional (*i.e.* accountancy and legal) advice, but lacks London's strength in shipping and commodities, while Chicago dominates in commodities and derivatives transactions. Zurich is strong on banking, investment, gold and insurance. Tokyo is prominent in banking and investment.

Wholesale Centre

London, like New York, has become almost a wholesale centre in financial services. By this we mean that in several areas, London and New York are attracting business from other financial centres. In the case of the City alone, it can be said that Singapore, Nassau, Bahrain and Hong Kong, for example, normally channel a significant amount of their financial business to London.

The best examples are:

(i) Re-insurance   The capacity of the London insurance market, made up of Lloyd's and the insurance and re-insurance companies, is so great that large risks accepted and arranged in other centres will to a large extent be re-insured in London. Countries which have nationalised their own insurance companies often re-insure their domestic risks, or a significant share of them, in London.

(ii) Euro-currency   While large international projects may well be arranged in regional centres such as Hong Kong or Singapore, the funds to finance them can often be sought in London. At the same time, local Euro-currency deposits from centres such as Singapore, running into billions of dollars, will also be deposited in London.

(iii) Shipping Fixtures   The Baltic Exchange will naturally attract shipping fixtures relating to British trade with South America, Africa and the Far East. In addition, shipowners in Tokyo, Los Angeles or

Rio de Janeiro will seek cargoes in London for journeys that do not touch British shores.

(iv) Commodities London's commodity markets attract business between commodity producing countries and third countries. It is estimated that this often accounts for half London's commodity turnover. The London Metal Exchange handles 90 per cent of the world's turnover.

(v) Foreign Exchange Banking demand in London to finance international banking transactions brings non-British business to the foreign exchange market. A larger share of trading in dollars and Deutschmarks takes place in London than in New York or Frankfurt respectively. The depth of the London exchange market also attracts arbitrage business from all over the world.

World Competition

London has been competing in the world financial market for centuries. In the eighteenth century, the main competitor was Amsterdam. In the nineteenth century, Paris and Berlin were the main competitors. In the twentieth century, New York was added to the list.

After 1945, New York and Zurich were in the forefront of the competition at the outset, with Tokyo becoming prominent later. Frankfurt has revived strongly in the past two decades. Paris has maintained its position. Regional newcomers in Singapore, Hong Kong and Nassau have developed well. So why has London remained so competitive so long? Several basic advantages have been maintained, as well as two fundamental post-war characteristics. The main advantages are:

(i) Political stability.
(ii) Good communications (airlines and telecommunications).
(iii) Time-zone (ability to deal with Far East and North America on same day).
(iv) Compactness (all markets within a Square Mile).
(v) Free economic and financial system.
(vi) Competition encouraged (large numbers of foreign banks, security houses, shipping firms and insurance companies).
(vii) Swift decisions (big deals based on trust or word of mouth).
(viii) World contacts (political and Commonwealth links maintained in post-war world).
(ix) Back-up of professional services (legal and accounting).

In addition, London has managed to maintain two essentials since 1945: the provision of money and continuing innovations.

Provision of Money

For a century and a half after the Napoleonic wars, London and the world were based on sterling. London could thus provide both money and financial services.

As the pound weakened in the 1940s and 1950s, London's sterling capital market began to dry up. It was at that precise moment that the City actively developed the Euro-currency market (see Chapter 10) and thus managed to replace the provision of pounds with the provision of Euro-currencies, *i.e.* other countries' currencies.

So although sterling finance is now well below dollar finance and probably, Deutschmark and yen finance, London-based banks can supply Euro-currencies of all kinds to support London-based services.

Innovation

Changes in the international financial markets have been quickening in the past decade. Innovation has spread quickly across frontiers. Technology has helped some of the changes; it has precipitated others. Legislation too (or its removal) has helped to change the structure of markets. These changes are still developing. London must keep pace if it is to maintain its competitive edge.

In the post-war period, London has produced several major innovations:

   (i) New air-freight market on Baltic Exchange (1949).
  (ii) Development of the Euro-currency and Eurobond markets (1958–60).
 (iii) Development of inter-bank wholesale market (1965–75).
 (iv) Unlisted securities market on Stock Exchange (1979–80).
  (v) Venture capital for small businesses (1976–84).
 (vi) Insurance cover for nuclear plants, satellites, industrial complexes.
(vii) Finance packages for international projects.
(viii) New international financial futures market: LIFFE (1982 onwards).
 (ix) New futures markets in petroleum, freight, etc. (1981–85), and new options markets (Stock Exchange and LIFFE).

   (x) Development of new Euro-currency techniques such as swaps, FRNs, RUFs and NIFs.

  (xi) Established London as a major fund management centre.

Future Changes

The biggest changes recently have taken place in banking, investment and in futures and derivatives. Controls on banking have been under review in Britain, the USA, Australia and Japan. Big structural changes in stock markets have taken place in London and Tokyo. And the European Union is still creating an internal financial market, free of restrictions, with open access to banks and financial institutions operating in member countries. And the new Euro currency has been launched.

As a result, the following broad changes will now bear watching:

   (i) The development of financial supermarkets, *i.e.* large groups providing a variety of services including banking, insurance, commodities and investment. This may lead to the gradual breakdown of barriers between different specialisations. Unlike the U.S. and Japan, where such barriers now seem to be breaking down, there is no statutory division in London between deposit banking and securities underwriting.

  (ii) Moves towards 24-hour global trading in securities, commodities, futures and derivatives by the establishment of firms in, or linkage of groups between, leading regional financial centres.

(iii) The development of new technologies providing global information, the transfer of money and the ability to deal in a variety of instruments and commodities. This is already having a profound impact on the trading floors of leading financial and commodity markets.

As we enter the third millennium, these basic influences are increasingly changing the face of London, New York, Frankfurt and Tokyo. Much bigger trading units are evolving, capable of undertaking a variety of different services on a global basis. Trading floors are giving way to computer screens. Individual financial centres are becoming more and more international. A world in which it will be possible to deal in most securities, commodities, derivatives and other financial instruments twenty four hours a day is getting nearer. London at least seems to be competing as vigorously as ever in this rapidly changing climate.

Global Trading in Foreign Exchange, Securities and Futures

What foreign exchange dealers have been doing for decades, security, futures and derivative traders are at last beginning to emulate. Global, "round-the-clock" trading is spreading rapidly into different markets and different market-places.

Investors' needs, reflecting the internationalisation of businesses, have coincided with two other phenomena: an increase in world communications (via satellites) and technology, and the de-regulation of financial markets. As a result, financial institutions are preparing themselves for global trading, in a variety of instruments, throughout 24 hours

- In the case of *foreign exchange dealings* (see Chapter 8 and Map A) these have straddled the world's time zones for some time, with London lying comfortably in the middle. London begins to deal before Tokyo has closed. As the map shows, New York and Los Angeles begin to deal in the middle of London's peak activity. They have an incentive to begin early and, when the exchanges are extremely active, dealers in New York and Los Angeles have been known to begin at 5.00 a.m. local time to coincide with London dealings.
- Since the introduction of changes in security dealings in London and Tokyo, global *trading in international securities* (see Map B) has been increasing—helped by satellite communications and new technology. Dealing times on individual stock exchanges are lengthening (in London, in New York and in Continental centres) in order to facilitate truly global transactions.
- Dealings in commodities have straddled the globe for decades. But only in recent years have *futures and derivatives transactions* (see Chapter 13 and Map C) begun to expand rapidly, linking one centre with another. As traditional markets (in Chicago and New York) and new markets (in London, Zurich, Frankfurt, Paris, Sydney, Montreal and Vancouver) have moved more closely together, global transactions have become more feasible.

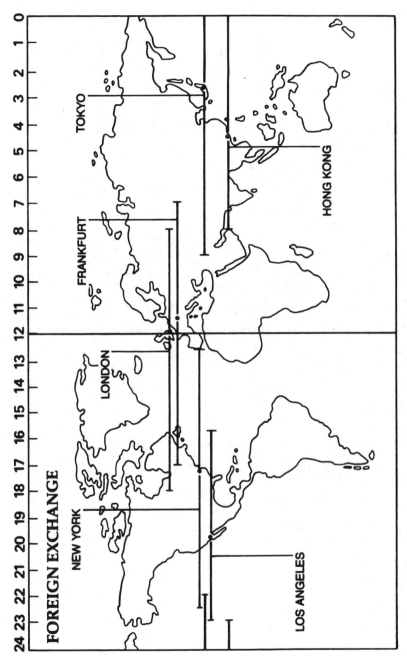

MAP A. *Global trading in FOREIGN EXCHANGE (all times shown in GMT)*

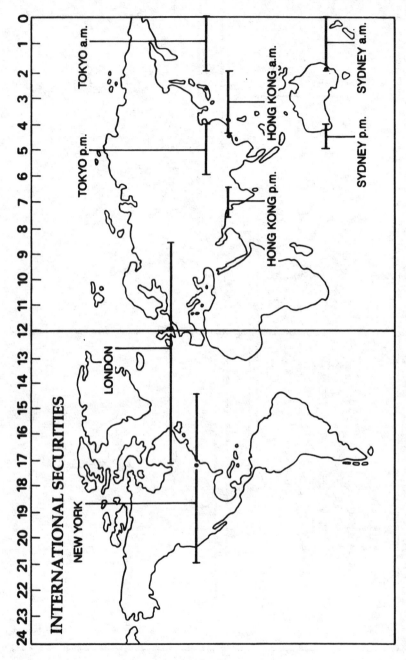

MAP B. Global trading in INTERNATIONAL SECURITIES (all times shown in GMT)

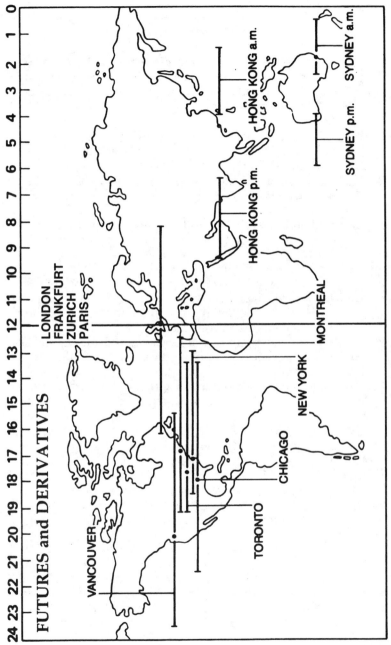

MAP C. Global trading in FUTURES and DERIVATIVES (all times shown in GMT)

127

Who Owns The City?

The obvious questions are not always the easiest to answer. Ownership of the City's main freeholds has in fact been changing throughout its history and is still going on. The historical process has briefly followed this pattern:

- When the Romans withdrew from the City in 410 A.D., they left an area of 330 acres enclosed by a wall (small sections still remaining) $3\frac{1}{4}$ miles long with 6 gates.
- The Great Fire of 1666 destroyed two thirds of the City. The area destroyed was about the same as in the Second World War.
- By 1700 London was the world's largest City, with the bulk of the country's imports and exports passing through it.
- The main commercial area in the 18th century was the warehouse district near the docks.
- Purpose-built offices started to emerge in the early 1820s. And further developments in the 19th century were stimulated by the completion of railway termini, the London Underground and the introdcution of the hydraulic lift.
- By 1914 *land ownership* in the City was still mainly in the hands of the aristocratic families, the Church, and the City's livery companies.
- The Corporation of London (in effect the local authority) only emerged as a significant land owner after the second World War.

The latest enquiry shows that no less than 20% of all property in the City is owned by foreign companies, that their stake has nearly trebled since 1983 and that over 35% of City offices are now occupied by foreign firms. *German companies have the largest share of ownership*, followed by Japanese and American companies. *American companies are the largest foreign occupiers* of office space.

This rise in foreign ownership of the City has coincided with the City's growing international status. It is in effect the essential cement to London's world role. The 20% of foreign involvement in the City compares with less than 5% in Frankfurt and Paris.

(*Source: Development Securities and Reading University.*)

16. How The City is Controlled

Financial markets should not be a free for all. The markets themselves need guidelines in order to function safely and efficiently. Users of the markets, whether small investors or professional institutions, need protection from fraud and malpractice. And the public sometimes needs reassurance that such markets are broadly in the public interest. So efficiency, protection and public policy have all been involved in building up the regulations for the City's financial markets.

In the days when traditional institutions, such as the merchant banks or stockbroking firms, were undertaking the bulk of the City's financial business, a combination of self-regulation, a limited statutory framework and Bank of England "nods and winks" were sufficient to keep the City reasonably under control. But as markets broadened, newcomers were introduced and new instruments and technologies began to spread, the need for stricter supervision grew stronger. A few frauds and collapses underlined the need for change. So, following a report from Professor Gower (in 1982), a new Securities and Investment Board (SIB) was eventually set up in 1988. This not only recognised and supervised five self-regulatory organisations, covering several City institutions, firms and markets, but also provided a framework for the regulation of investment firms. Its broad supervisory role was shared by the Bank of England, Lloyd's, the Department of Trade and the Treasury.

After close on a decade's experience of such statutory regulation, with City failures, scandals and financial upsets continuing, it was decided to bring all the regulatory bodies more closely together under one umbrella. The SIB was replaced by the new Financial Services Authority (FSA) and a new Parliamentary Act establishing the details of its powers is promised by the year 2000. In preparation for the detail the FSA is now established in new quarters in Canary Wharf (see Chapter 1).

In effect the FSA will be the single regulator of all the City institutions. It has already taken over the Bank of England's supervisory role over banks, and over the foreign exchange, derivative and bullion markets. It has absorbed the staff of several professional bodies as well as the Insurance Directorate of the Treasury. In addition three self-regulating organisations have transferred their staff and their operational functions to the FSA. These are the SFA (the Securities and Futures Authority), IMRO (the Investment Management Regulatory Organisation) and PIA (the Personal Investment Authority). Between them these three cover fund management firms, investment trusts, unit trusts, portfolio managers, financial advisers, sellers of personal pensions funds, and the Eurobond, financial futures and commodity futures markets. Lloyd's will also come under the FSA umbrella.

The four basic objectives of the FSA are:

- To maintain confidence in the U.K.'s financial markets;
- To protect the consumers of financial services;
- To promote consumer understanding of the risks and benefits of financial services;
- To reduce the extent to which financial firms are used for the purpose of financial crime.

As I write it is too soon to assess how the latest attempt at statutory regulation will work. The SFA has had to absorb a variety of other regulators under one roof; it has had to consider integrating different codes of conduct, to iron out conflicting lines of supervision, and to initiate new ones. It has absorbed remarkable new powers, including immunity from prosecution, but is not entirely free from outside curbs (the appeal arrangements should see to that).

Two earlier regulators of different parts of the City, however, still retain certain important responsibilities. The Bank of England remains responsible for the overall stability of the financial system and for the efficiency and effectiveness of the financial sector, including playing a leading role in promoting the City. Moreover, the Treasury remains fully responsible for the overall institutional structure of regulation and the legislation which governs it. Although the Treasury has no operative responsibility for either the Bank of England or the FSA, both have an obligation to give the Treasury an alert about possible problems: in cases which might lead to economic disruption; where official financial support might be needed; where diplomatic issues might arise; where changes in law may be needed; and where questions in the House of Commons are involved.

The main questions remain: in future will the FSA be able to stave off such events as the BCCI collapse, the Baring's failure, the Maxwell

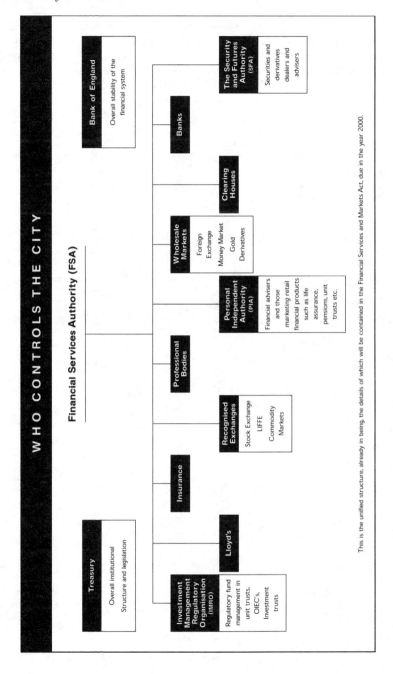

WHO CONTROLS THE CITY

Financial Services Authority (FSA)

Treasury
Overall institutional Structure and legislation

Bank of England
Overall stability of the financial system

Investment Management Regulatory Organisation (IMRO)
Regulatory fund management in unit trusts, OIEC's, Investment trusts

| Lloyd's |

| Insurance |

Recognised Exchanges
Stock Exchange LIFFE Commodity Markets

| Professional Bodies |

Personal Independent Authority (PIA)
Financial advisers and those *marketing* retail financial products such as life assurance, pensions, unit trusts etc.

Wholesale Markets
Foreign Exchange Money Market Gold Derivatives

| Clearing Houses |

| Banks |

The Security and Futures Authority (SFA)
Securities and derivatives dealers and advisers

This is the unified structure, already in being, the details of which will be contained in the Financial Services and Markets Act, due in the year 2000.

affair, the Guiness take-over of Argyll, the Blue Arrow affair, the multi-million pound pensions mis-selling scandal and the millions lost in derivative transactions? Or will it be so keen to do so that it strangles the City's foreign earnings' potential in a mass of red tape?

17. Glossary

Technical terms, or jargon, naturally dominate the City of London. We have tried to explain individual terms in each chapter as they have occurred. This glossary, introduced for the first time in this edition, is an attempt to put them together for ready reference, or as a reminder of earlier explanations.

Several things are worth remembering. Jargon used in one section of the City, may not be fully understood in another. Shipping and insurance use language and shorthand of their own. A banker may not be too familiar with "charterparties" or "retrocession insurance". The stock market too has its own jargon of "bears", "bulls" and "redemption yields".

Jargon also changes over time and from place to place. What intrigued Dickens ("things that go up and down in the City") may be described differently nowadays. And what is instantly recognised in New York, may be called something else again in London. This glossary, therefore, is a simple attempt to include technical terms in current use in the City of London in the 1990s. No more, no less.

Acceptances Short-term, fixed interest loans, based upon bills of exchange, drawn on a bank, the bills being discounted at market rates. Acceptances are normally related to a company's trading activities.

Annuity This is a form of life assurance that, like a pension, provides for a sum of money to be paid at regular intervals to the policyholder.

Arbitrage Dealings in foreign exchange, securities or other instruments with the aim of making profits out of the differences in exchange rates, security prices or other prices existing in different centres or at different times.

Bearer Bond Bonds for which ownership is shown by a document rather than an entry in a register. Title is transferred by delivery of the bearer document.

Bear market A "bear" is an investor who sells shares (often those he does not possess) in the hope that prices will fall, thereby enabling him to buy more cheaply later. The same intention applies to "bears" of individual currencies or commodities. Thus a "bear market" is a period of falling prices. Technicians and chartists have formulae for recognising such markets.

Bill-broker He was originally a middle-man who helped others to buy or sells bills of exchange for a commission. Nowadays the term is used in a wider context to include individuals and firms that make a market in bills of exchange, Treasury bills and other money market instruments.

Bills of exchange These are essentially paper promises, signed by one person requiring a second person or firm to pay a certain sum of money on demand or on a fixed date, normally short-term. They are, in effect, post-dated cheques. They were defined by the Bills of Exchange Act of 1882. Such bills, when "accepted", can be sold for cash to discount houses.

Bill on London A bill of exchange issued in any part of the world, but "accepted" in London. This was the traditional method of sterling finance throughout the nineteenth century and later.

Blue chip A high quality industrial share. The term is said to be of American origin, derived from the colour of the highest value poker chip.

Big Bang Usually refers to the major changes on the London Stock Exchange on October 27, 1986, when major innovations in the method of buying and selling shares as well as in the ownership of firms were introduced overnight.

Broker/dealer A member of the London Stock Exchange who provides advice and dealing services to the public. They may intermediate between customers and market-makers and may also act as principals, transacting business with customers from their own holdings of stock.

Broking houses Traditionally such firms acted middle-men, linking sellers and buyers in commodities, money, foreign exchange, securities, shipping freights, gold, etc., in exchange for a commission. Nowadays they often buy and sell as principals on their own account, depending on the habits and regulations within their particular trade.

Bull market A "bull" is an investor who buys shares now, with cash or credit, in the hope that prices will rise in the future so that he can make a profit. A "bull market" is thus a period of rising share prices. Similar attitudes towards currencies or commodities are likewise described as "bullish". Technicians have formulae for recognising "bull" markets.

Call money These are cash deposits placed by banks with discount houses which can be withdrawn on demand.

Call option The right to buy stock, shares or other commodity at an agreed price at a future date.

Capital base Basically this is the capital employed in a business, including capital reserves, loans and ordinary shares.

Capital issue The issue of securities with a view to raising capital for a company.

Capitalisation issue The process whereby money from a company's reserves is converted into issued capital, which is then distributed to shareholders as new shares, in proportion to their original holdings. Also known as *bonus issue* or *scrip issue*.

Captive insurance company An insurance company established by a company, trade association or other non-insurance organisation, primarily for the insurance and/or re-insurance of the founder's (or its members') own risks.

Certificates of Deposit (or CD's) Certificates given to a lender of funds by a bank, which can then be traded in the market to realise the cash assets. This enables the bank to hold the funds for a guaranteed period of time, while the lender is free to trade the CD's whenever he wishes.

Charter party An agreement drawn up between the two sides of a shipping contract—the owners of the ship and the cargo to be carried.

Clearing House Normally used in banking where cheques are cleared and credited to appropriate accounts. The term is also used in the commodity and derivative trades where a clearing house provides a guarantee of payments to participants.

Commercial bills Bills of exchange issued by commercial companies, which can be accepted or endorsed by banks (and then referred to as "bank bills") or *not* accepted by banks (in which case they are referred to as "trade bills").

Convertibility Usually referring to currencies. A "convertible currency" is one which monetary authorities allow the holders to switch freely into other currencies or gold.

Coupon Annual interest usually paid on gilt-edge stock, for example, in two equal, semi-annual instalments. Expressed as a percentage of the nominal value of the stock.

Cover The amount of money a company has available for distribution as dividend, divided by the amount actually paid gives the number of times that the dividend is *covered*.

Debenture A document issued under a trust deed that creates or acknowledges a debt. It usually relates to a security transaction payable within a specified period, carries a fixed rate of interest and is secured against the general assets of a company.

Derivative A term that embraces futures, forwards, options and warrants, *i.e.* financial instruments that are based on a real asset, such as a commodity, a currency or money of any kind. Derivatives can be based on standard products traded under the rules of an exchange or customised products traded "over the counter".

Discount Houses Companies that specialise in discounting bills of exchange, Treasury bills, etc., and in dealing in short-dated Government bonds. The "discounting" of a bill implies the offer of cash for it below its face value. This discount is a reflection of the current rate of interest, the quality of the bill and its maturity date.

Discount When the market price of a newly issued security is lower than the issue price. If it is higher, the difference is called a *premium*.

Endowment policies A combination of life assurance and investment whereby the sum assured is payable on a predetermined date or on prior death.

Equity This is another name for Ordinary shares, which provide that the ultimate ownership of companies should carry votes at all general meetings of companies and thus control overall policy. An equity stake in a company carries with it the ownership of the company, carrying with it the right to a share in profits and the risk of bearing losses.

Eurobond   These are bonds or notes with a final maturity, with either a fixed or floating interest rate, issued in a Eurocurrency. Originally the buyer of the bond or note usually held it outside the country of origin of the currency in which it was denominated. With increased currency and other freedoms, this distinction has now become blurred.

Eurocurrency   The name given to any currency, held outside its country of origin, *e.g.* Euro-dollar, Euro-sterling, Euro-yen, Euro-mark, etc. The "Euro" appelation derives from the place where the first market in such external currencies (primarily dollars) actually arose. Not to be confused with the new European currency, the Euro.

Factoring   This is a service, provided by a third party to companies, which includes sales accounting, debt-collection services and protection against bad debts. Customers also receive immediate payments for a high percentage of debts owed to them.

Fixture   The name given to the final details of a shipping agreement between a shipowner and the owner of the cargo. Once agreement is reached, the ship is said to be "fixed". Hence the name.

Floating rates   Rates of interest calculated as a fixed margin above a variable rate of interest such as that in Singapore, London or other Interbank Offered Rate (see LIBOR). They are normally used in Euro-currency loans or Eurobonds (known as Floating Rate Notes).

Flotation   The occasion on which a company's shares are offered on the stock market for the first time.

Footsie   A coloquial reference to the FT-SE 100 Share Index of 100 leading U.K. shares listed on the London Stock Exchange. Started on January 3, 1984. It is the basis of a traded option contract.

Foreign bond issues   Bonds issued on a domestic market on behalf of foreign borrowers, corporate or Government. The distinction between them and Eurobonds as become blurred.

Forfaiting This is a form of supplier's credit ranging from six months to five years and beyond. It is usually based on a bill of exchange or a promissory note.

Forward market A market in forward contracts of a commodity or currency or financial instrument, which are agreements to sell or purchase a certain agreed amount at a future date. Unlike futures contracts such contracts cannot be transferred or sold to second or third parties.

FT Index This is the original *Financial Times* share index of 30 leading industrial shares on the London market, begun in 1935.

Futures market A market in futures contracts which basically requires the delivery of a commodity, currency or security in a specified future month, if not liquidated before that date. They can be transferred to third parties and thus traded in.

Gearing Basically this is the proportional relationship between debt capital (plus borrowing) and equity capital. Changes in this proportion can be used to increase or decrease the risk of profit or loss.

GEMM These are gilt-edged market makers, *i.e.* dealers in Government securities who are required to make continuous two-way prices on request to any member of the London Stock Exchange and to investors known to them directly.

Gilt-edged stock Fixed interest securities issued and guaranteed by the British Government. The term is sometimes used to include U.K. local authority securities and Commonwealth government securities. "Gilt-edged" derives from the original use of high quality paper with gilt edges on the earliest certificates. Term said to have been used for first time in 1892. "Long gilts" are issues without a redemption date within 15 years; "medium gilts" are those with a redemption between 7 and 15 years; and "short gilts" are those with a redemption date within 7 years.

Gold standard The international monetary system in operation generally throughout the nineteenth century and up to 1931. A country was said to be on the Gold Standard when its currency was based on an agreed amount of gold, when it agreed to buy and sell gold at fixed prices and when gold could be moved in and out freely.

Government Broker Formerly he was a stockbroker appointed to act as the Government's agent in the gilt-edged market. Traditionally he was the senior partner of Mullens & Co. Since "Big Bang" he has been a senior Bank of England official, who advises and acts for the National Debt Office, and acts as adviser to the Government.

Index linked gilt   A Government security whose interest and capital change in line with the official Retail Price Index.

Hedging   A method of insuring against price fluctuations through the purchase of a futures contract. A "hedge" can be the establishment of an opposite position in the futures market to that held in the spot or physical market.

Hedge funds   They usually employ the use of derivatives instruments to enhance risks rather than to offset them.

Hot money   Short term money that moves from one financial centre to another and is quickly affected by changes in exchange rates, interest rates, economic policies or simply monetary fears.

Instalment credit   A form of personal or industrial credit under which the ownership of the goods or equipment passes to the borrower on the repayment of an agreed number of instalments.

Institutional investors   The large financial institutions such as insurance companies, pension funds, unit and investment trusts, etc., in contrast to private investors.

Insurance brokers   Specialised and officially recognised brokers who secure insurance business and place it with recognised underwriters.

Interbank market   Financial transactions between banks, often forming a base for quotations of rates for commercial borrowing from banks.

Investment trust   A company that invests a fixed amount of money in a variety of stocks and shares, thus providing a way of spreading risks. They have fixed capital, unlike unit trusts which can create or redeem units in response to demand. They are therefore referred to as "closed-end funds". The price is regulated by the supply and demand for shares and does not necessarily reflect the underlying asset value.

Invisible exports or income   Foreign income from sources other than the movement of physical goods (visible exports). Invisible income is thus derived from the sale of services to foreigners and from the interest, profits and dividends derived from the ownership of foreign investments.

Jobbers   These were members of the London Stock Exchange before Big Bang who acted as market-makers in shares and traded as principals on their own account. They could only deal with brokers not the general public.

Leads and lags   A phrase used to describe deliberate delays in payments in certain currencies and accelerate payment in others, in efforts by international traders to protect themselves against exchange rate fluctuations.

Leasing   Facilities provided under equipment-leasing agreements by banks or their subsidiaries. The assets being financed remain in the ownership of the leasing company but are effectively hired out to the customer.

Libor   London Interbank Offered Rate. The rate of interest used as the basis of lending in the Eurocurrency markets.

Life Offices   Firms that assure the payment of agreed sums of money on a given date or on death, in return for the payment of regular premiums. They can be mutual offices (owned by with-profits policyholders), proprietary companies (owned by shareholders) or friendly societies.

Listed company   A company that has obtained permission for its shares to be admitted to the London Stock Exchange.

Loan stock   A generic term covering securities issued against loans.

Long   To be "long" of a commodity, security or currency implies having a surplus of it.

Market capitalisation   The current stock market valuation of a company's outstanding capital.

Merchant bank   Was formerly the name given to members of the Accepting Houses Committee, whose bills had special privileges at the Bank of England. Now used as a broader description of investment houses in London, offering both banking and security services, as well as a variety of other services.

Minimum Lending Rate (MLR) This weekly rate, imposed by the Bank of England, replaced the old Bank Rate in London in October 1972. Its use was later discontinued in practice, though it remains in reserve.

Name The term used to describe members of Lloyd's, the insurance market.

Net asset value The value of a company after all debts have been paid, expressed in pence per share.

Offshore centre A financial centre free of many taxes and constraints. The term was first applied to literally "offshore" centres of the U.S. such as the Bahamas, Cayman Islands, etc. It can also refer to certain international transactions in a city like New York, Tokyo or London that are specially free of normal domestic taxes and rules.

Option market Markets in entitlements to trade in underlying share or commodity at a fixed price at any time within a specified period. The buyer of the option pays a premium for the guarantee of receiving or delivering the security or commodity at the fixed price until the option expires.

Ordinary shares Holders of Ordinary shares (also known as the equity) in a company are the owners of a company, and have the right to vote at company meetings. They are the risk capital of a company benefitting from success and, at the same time, risking ultimate loss.

Outcry market A market which is based on competitive bids expressed by participants in person. Sometimes referred to as "rings", as in the London Metal Exchange.

Overdraft The traditionally British form of bank loan. The borrower agrees a maximum limit and can then draw up to this amount from his account. He is charged on the amount he uses. It is usually repayable on demand.

Overnight money Money lent for one day up to 3 p.m. that will be automatically repaid the following business day.

Parallel money market Name originally given to markets in money, in both sterling and foreign currencies, that grew up alongside the traditional money market.

Pension funds   Funds created to finance the provision of pensions to employees.

P and I Clubs   Mutual indemnity associations of ship-owners, charterers, etc., to protect themselves against certain liability and other marine risks not normally covered by marine insurers.

Portfolio investment   Investment in securities, in contrast with investment in fixed assets such as factories, property, etc.

Preference shares   These are normally fixed-income shares, whose holders have the right to receive dividends before Ordinary shares but after debenture and loan stock holders have received their interest.

Prices/Earnings Ratio   The current share price divided by the last published earnings. It is used as a measure of whether a share should be considered "expensive" or not.

Primary market   A market that deals in newly issued shares, in contrast to a secondary market which deals in existing securities.

Redemption date   The date on which a security is due to be repaid by the issuer at its full face value.

Re-insurers   Insurance companies that help to spread risks by accepting insurance business from other insurance companies and underwriters.

Retrocession   The re-insurance of claims liabilities incurred under contracts of re-insurance.

Roll-over   Describes a method of extending the maturity of a loan.

SEAQ   The London Stock Exchange's Automated Quotation system for U.K. securities.

SEAQ International   The London Stock Exchange's electronic screen system for non-U.K. equities.

Secondary market   A place for buying and selling *existing* securities, in contrast to the primary market which deals in *new* securities.

Short   To be "short" of a commodity, a security or a currency implies having oversold it.

Spot market   A market in actual goods for immediate delivery.

Stag   An investor who applies for a new issue in the hope of being able to sell the shares allotted to him at a profit as soon as dealing starts.

Swap   A financial instrument that enables participants to exchange one kind of obligation for another, usually in relation to interest rates or exchange rates, on agreed terms. Swaps form part of the derivative market.

Syndicate   A group of people or of institutions that come together with a specific purpose, such as a group of banks putting together a Euro-syndicated loan, or a group within Lloyd's pooling resources to cover insurance risks.

Tender offer   In an offer by tender, buyers of shares specify the price at which they are willing to buy.

Term loan   A bank loan for a fixed amount and for an agreed length of time, in contrast to the traditional overdraft.

Term policy   This is a type of insurance policy that provides for an agreed sum of money to be paid to the policyholder's family or next of kin but only if the policyholder happens to die within an agreed period of time.

Treasury bill   Promissory note issued by the Treasury, usually for 91 days, to finance Government expenditure short-term.

Underwriter   An insurer or an individual who decides what risks to accept and on what terms.

Unit Trust   A fund of stocks and shares held by a trustee for the benefit of subscribing investors. They offer a means of spreading risks. Since new units can be created or redeemed, they are referred to as "open-ended" funds.

Venture Capital   In contrast to normal bank loans to small businesses, this is based on the supply of equity capital (plus loan capital) and management expertise. The hope is that the company offering the capital will be able to "float" the company's shares on the stock market in due course.

Wall Street   The financial district of New York in Lower Manhattan. The American equivalent of "the City".

Warrant   A special kind of option, given by the company to holders of a particular security, giving them the right to subscribe for future issues, either of the same kind or some other security.

Whole life policy   This provides for an agreed sum of money to be paid to the policyholder's family or next of kin when the policyholder dies, whenever that may be.

Yield   The annual return on money invested, based on the current price of a security, on the assumption that the next dividend will be the same as the last one. *Flat yield* is the income on a fixed interest stock, ignoring any capital gain that may be made if the stock is due to be redeemed at par at some future date. *Redemption yield* is the same, but allowing for the expected capital gain.

Index